CULTURAL
SENSITIVITY
TRAINING

"*Intercultural competency is one of the top skills that employers seek. **Cultural Sensitivity Training** provides a simple, yet elegant framework to help readers navigate the cultural minefield in our global work world. It's loaded with exercises and resources that help students and experienced business leaders work more successfully with culturally diverse colleagues. I highly recommend this great and timely book.*"

Dr Carol Scovotti, Arno Kleimenhagen Professor of Marketing,
University of Wisconsin-Whitewater (USA)

"*Susann Kowalski's book is essential reading for anyone who would like to improve their communication style in multilingual and multinational settings. This book will significantly increase your self-awareness and knowledge around intercultural communication issues. It gives a really useful broad and deep synopsis of the main models and theories and provides superb practical advice and guidance. A great piece of work!*"

Dr Alexandra Morgan, Author of *Coaching International Teams: Improving Communication, Inclusion and Productivity* (UK)

"*Navigating differences is a much-needed skill in today's complex world. This book provides practical and accessible exercises for supporting readers in navigating some of these differences, helping them build their intercultural competence.*"

Dr Darla Deardorff, Research Fellow (Social Science Research Institute), Duke University (USA), author of *Manual on Developing Intercultural Competence: Story Circles* and other books

"*This book puts together the theoretical framework about intercultural communication in a unique perspective. This is an amazing book and an added value to the intercultural communication educational library.*"

Dr Eva Haddad Al-Faraj, Assistant Professor SBSH, German Jordanian University (Jordan)

SUSANN KOWALSKI

CULTURAL SENSITIVITY
TRAINING

Developing the Basis for Effective
Intercultural Communication

econcise
Concise books for smart learners

Our mission at econcise publishing
is to create concise, approachable and affordable
textbooks for a new generation of smart learners.

Paperback ISBN: 978-3-903386-13-6
ePub ISBN: 978-3-903386-14-3
Kindle ISBN: 978-3-903386-15-0

Cover image and 'globe' icon: iStock.com/Glopphy
Autor image (back cover): Susann Kowalski
Illustration elements:
  • p. 3: iStock/HerminUtomo
  • p. 12: pixabay.com, iStock/Guzaliia Filimonova
  • p. 91: pixabay.com, iStock/Dreamcreation

First published 2023 by **econcise publishing**
© 2023 econcise GmbH
Am Sonnengrund 14
A-9062 Moosburg (Austria)

www.econcise.com

Contents

5 Reach out: Taking your intercultural competence to the next level

Introduction

Cultural sensitivity is the conscious perception of cultural differences. It is the basis for all culturally appropriate action, the development of intercultural competence, and successful intercultural communication.

Developing your cultural sensitivity will help you to recognize the diversity of people's values, perceptions, and attitudes, and then actively harness this diversity to find creative solutions, in cross-cultural encounters as well as within your own cultural environment. Thus, cultural sensitivity can also contribute to resolving supposedly irreconcilable viewpoints or positions.

If you haven't studied a formal course on intercultural competence, intercultural communication, or intercultural management yet, you can use this book as a standalone way of acquiring basic skills for dealing with people from other cultures. If you are currently studying such a course, this book can provide you with an additional perspective on what you are learning (including a range of practical exercises that will help you develop your skills to the next level).

Maybe you are already working in a culturally diverse team or are even being sent to another country for the first time in your career? In this case, the exercises in this book will help prepare you to make sense of the cross-cultural differences you will encounter. You will also learn about a few basic reaction patterns that you will observe in others as well as in yourself.

If you are a lecturer, teacher, or trainer, this book will provide you with ideas for how to enrich your lessons with intercultural aspects and practical exercises that will prepare your students for a diverse work environment.

The chapters in this book build on each other. I would therefore recommend you work through it step by step. Afterward, you can pick out and practice individual exercises that you find particularly helpful or enlightening for your specific situation. If you use the book to accompany a course, then simply pick out the parts that fit the course contents.

The best way to use this book is to work through it together with a friend, colleague, or fellow student, or in a small group of three to four people. Many exercises are based on comparing your own position or perspective with that of others. Of course, it is also possible to use the book for self-study and I provide some hints for 'solo learners' in the exercise descriptions.

For years, I have been teaching intercultural competence, communication, and management in my home country of Germany as well as in many other countries around the world. During this time, I have realized that since we never know which countries our students will end up living or working in during their professional careers, teaching 'dos and don'ts' for a few selected countries is neither sufficient nor appropriate. As soon as students came to a country that had not been included in the program, they would still not be prepared.

I have also noticed that at the beginning of their studies, many students still adhere to the idea that there are no cultural differences at all, or that one should overlook these differences and instead consider the commonalities only. Sooner or later, however, not paying attention to the differences will lead to problems. If we are unable to see the differences, we will also fail to unlock the potential that lies within them.

If you are, in contrast, able to develop a feeling for where differences might hide, and if you perceive these differences as inspiring, you can start building on them and actively look for creative solutions when conflicts are emerging.

This book will prepare you for any diverse intercultural situation regardless of the specific cultural context. The advice given here has already been tested and refined with several generations of students.

When I asked my students to express in one sentence what they had learned by the end of the course on developing cultural sensitivity that

I've been teaching at my home university, I heard phrases like:

- *"I learned that my behavior depends on my cultural background."*
- *"Having an open mind and accepting other cultures are the baselines for successful intercultural communication."*
- *"The world can look different from the perspective of another person— and it is still true."*
- *"The best way to look at a country is through the eyes of its people."*
- *"Being open-minded toward other people and their cultures gives you the chance to develop a respectful communication base when working with international partners."*
- *"Adaptability is hard, but when you get there, it's an amazing feeling."*

Through reading this book, you will soon be able to make such statements for yourself. To this end, this book will guide you through a **cultural sensitivity training** with the following five steps (see also Figure 1).

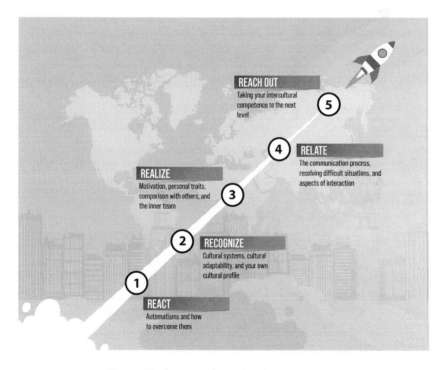

Figure 1 The five steps of our cultural sensitivity training

- In **Chapter 1** ('**React**'), we will take a look at the automatic reaction patterns which are inherent in humans and assess to what extent they are helpful or harmful. We will discuss how we can consciously override these automatisms. We will also explore the effect of being part of different groups and why we automatically prefer our own group. This includes a consideration of stereotypes and what we need them for, as well as their negative effects.

- In **Chapter 2** ('**Recognize**'), we will get into some theoretical basics. We will take a look at different ways of categorizing cultural characteristics and explore why there are so many different classification systems. We will try to understand how we can use such categorizations to develop our cultural sensitivity, and why it could potentially also be dangerous to classify people by their culture. Furthermore, you will get the chance to explore your own cultural background and create your 'cultural repository.'

- In **Chapter 3** ('**Realize**'), you will be able to apply the insights from the first two chapters to your own personal situation. You will compare your cultural background and personality traits with other people's cultural backgrounds and personality traits, identify similarities and differences, and assess the opportunities and risks that lie in these differences.

- In **Chapter 4** ('**Relate**'), I will suggest a few tools that you can use to examine conflict situations from different perspectives and understand their causes. This will form the basis for resolving conflicts, and it's also a good starting point for successful intercultural communication. In this chapter, we will discover the requirements for successful communication in intercultural situations.

- **Chapter 5** ('**Reach out**') will provide you with additional ideas for developing your cultural sensitivity to a higher level. We will take a look at Milton Bennett's developmental model of intercultural sensitivity (DMIS), and you will assess which level of intercultural sensitivity you have already achieved yourself. This will help you develop a step-by-step plan for reaching your goal of becoming fully proficient in intercultural sensitivity and communication. I will suggest several options for your further development in this field of competence, from which you can then choose to devise your own development plan.

Taken together, the five chapters of this book will provide you with a solid overview of what cultural differences mean, how you can recognize them, and how they can be harnessed to find more creative solutions to problems that arise when people from different cultures interact and cooperate.

By the end of this book, you will know how to train your cultural sensitivity, strengthen your intercultural skills, and communicate more confidently across cultures.

I very much hope that this book will help you to experience cultural diversity as something that enriches your work and life, and that you will be able to use it proactively—for your career as well as for having rewarding encounters with people from all parts of the world.

P.S. In this book, you will learn how to better deal with differences between people, how to use those differences for creative problem solving, and how to better include people in your work and life along the way. To maintain a clear focus on developing your cultural sensitivity skills, I do not explicitly address the political dimensions of discrimination, racism, exclusion or inclusion, and existing power relations that perpetuate injustice. The skills that you will learn in this book, however, will help you promote inclusion and mitigate injustice at the individual level—and that might even be a small contribution to a better worldwide understanding of justice, which always starts on an individual level.

ACCESS FREE BONUS LEARNING MATERIALS

Check out the companion website of this book (*www.econcise.com/ CulturalSensitivityTraining*) for the following bonus learning materials:

- Use **templates** and **hints** for some of the exercises in this book.
- Download a **free mind map** that provides a succinct, visual 'big picture' overview of the key concepts from this book.
- All weblinks mentioned throughout the book are compiled in a **list of weblinks with commentary**.
- If you are a lecturer who wants to use this book for teaching purposes, we can provide you with **free, editable Microsoft PowerPoint slides** that you can use in your course (just send us an email to *lecturerservice@econcise.com* to get them).
- If you want to stay informed about current developments in the field and get more information about new books for smart leaders and learners, you are also welcome to **subscribe to our newsletter** at *www.econcise.com/newsletter*!

React: Automatisms and how to overcome them

This chapter enables you to:

» Describe why and how cultural values, attitudes, and beliefs evolve.
» Recognize the danger of stereotypes and bias.
» Become aware of your automatic reactions and how you can consciously influence them.

Are we all susceptible to stereotyping and favoring our own group? Do we think that we are 'better' than others? Do we all fear what is foreign to us? If you are answering these questions by saying, "Yes, that's just how people are," you are quite right in a way. There are automatic processes that trigger these behaviors and feelings, but what is important (and fundamental to this book) is that we are able to step in and control these automatic processes. We are, in fact, able to recognize them, slow them down, and consciously intervene.

The Austrian neurologist, psychiatrist and philosopher Viktor Frankl once said that there is always a space between stimulus and reaction, and that in that space, we have the power to choose our response. He concluded that in our reaction lies our development and our freedom.[1]

If you understand the **automatic processes** that are going on in our brains, and if you know how you can 'overrule' your automatic reactions and act differently, you can prevent the negative effects of these processes from happening. That is exactly what this chapter is about.

I will first introduce you to some of the key automatic processes (or 'automatisms') in our brain. These processes also determine our reactions in intercultural situations. We will then take a look at their advantages, as well as the unpleasant effects they can lead to, especially in the context of intercultural encounters. Finally, I will explain how you can interrupt these automatisms. In the following chapters, we will discuss strategies for replacing inadequate automatic reactions with more effective, conscious ways of dealing with cultural differences.

Automatisms in response to cultural differences

The evolutionary function of groups

Imagine living in a hunter-gatherer society tens of thousands of years ago. Your primary concerns are finding food and shelter, staying safe, and raising the next generation. There is no housing. Obviously, supermarkets are not available yet. And various animals are interested in you as their next meal. Can you manage all of this by yourself? Probably not.

You need other people to cooperate with, so that you can work together to search for food, find shelter, protect yourselves from attackers, and raise your children. The better you stand together as a group, the greater your chances of succeeding in the struggle for survival. Your own group offers safety and has to be defended against other groups. This leads to an 'us versus them' attitude. Group formation, therefore, has an **evolutionary function** (among others).[2]

As a single individual, you have your own interests, values, attitudes, and beliefs. But you also consider yourself as a member of the group. You know that you have obligations toward your group, and you are also prepared to act for the good of the group. Alongside your personal identity comes a **social or group identity**.[3] You follow and adopt the values, attitudes, and beliefs of the group you live in.

Nowadays, we do not need groups for our basic survival as urgently as we did several tens of thousands of years ago. Nevertheless, the basic mechanisms are still at work. Even today, we feel a sense of belonging to the groups in which we live or spend large parts of our time, and we adopt their values, attitudes, and beliefs. This leads to the concept of **culture**, which we will take a look at in more detail below.

In today's world, there are also additional influences from society. These are **social structures, laws, and institutions** through which you also learn and adopt values, attitudes, and beliefs. Society still follows—at least unconsciously—an 'us versus them' attitude. This results in certain areas of tension which explain some of the phenomena that occur in connection with intercultural encounters.

Categorization and stereotypes

Our environment is complex—too complex for us to perceive and process all the details.[4] Indeed, processing all the details would distort our view of the essentials and make it difficult to separate the important from the less important. It would also consume time and resources that we can make better use of for other vital life tasks.

Therefore, we automatically generalize and assign things or people we observe to categories. This process is called **categorization**. As soon as we notice that a thing or person fulfills a few easily perceivable characteristic features of a category, we mentally put this thing or person into a 'box'. We then simply transfer many other 'typical' characteristics of that particular category to this thing or person.

Susan Fiske and Steven Neuberg described this process in a **continuum model of impression formation**.[5] The model represents how we form impressions of people. The process begins with the automatic categorization (**automatic information processing**) just described. Only when it is necessary, and when we consciously initiate it, we can break this categorization and consciously perceive and process further information about the thing or person (**controlled information processing**).

This process of automatic categorization works as efficiently today as it did tens of thousands of years ago. It helps us to cope efficiently with our environment, but it also leads to stereotypes and, based on them, to prejudice and bias.

There's nothing inherently wrong with stereotypes. They are ideas that members of one group have about themselves (**auto-stereotypes**) or other groups (**hetero-stereotypes**). You can also hold stereotypes about yourself (**self-stereotypes**).

Stereotypes only become problematic when they lead to overly strong generalizations, and when they are associated with an evaluation about the other person. Negative stereotypes, in particular, hinder people from connecting with each other. They usually lead to discrimination and racism. We will talk about this in more detail below.

Fast reactions to protect against danger

Let's consider again our hunter-gatherer society. At that time, it was important to decide quickly whether or not a thing, animal, or human being posed a danger to you. A wrong decision could mean death. Whoever decided wrong once too often was likely not able to survive and pass on their slow reaction times to their ancestors.

When it came to encounters with other people, effectively deciding what action to take was based on your ability to quickly assess, based on a few external characteristics, whether the person you encountered belonged to your own group or a foreign one. An overcautious response could be lifesaving here, particularly when the other person was also fighting for their survival.

Thus, fast decisions based on little information have proven to be evolutionarily helpful. The Israeli-American psychologist and economist Daniel Kahneman together with his colleague, the Israeli psychologist and cognitive scientist Amos Tversky, speaks of the **fast mode of decision making** or 'System 1' thinking.[6] He contrasts it with the **slow mode of decision making** or 'System 2' thinking. In the latter case, the rapidly absorbed information is reviewed, supplemented by further information, and consciously processed, followed by a thoughtful (rather than just automatic) reaction.

While Fiske and Neuberg's continuum model of impression formation specifically focuses on human perception, Kahneman's fast and slow thinking model is more generally applicable.

Even today, it is still helpful to be able to react quickly to avert danger—for example when crossing a busy road or catching a toddler as they fall over. In social interactions, however, this can lead to detrimental reactions. If we do not switch to slow thinking here, this can lead to discrimination or even racism.

Dealing with cognitive dissonance

Another automatic mechanism is cognitive dissonance. You have probably experienced more than once something that turned out to be completely different from what you expected it to be. Maybe you studied a lot for an exam, answered all the practice questions well, and therefore expected a good grade. But your actual grade was much worse than you thought it would be. Perhaps you dwelled on that as you wrestled with your expectations versus reality.

We can also experience such 'wrestling of thoughts' when we meet people with different values and attitudes to what we expected them to have. This can hit us particularly hard if we perceive the other person's attitude as 'better' than our own, because we then feel our self-worth is being attacked.

The US social psychologist Leon Festinger called conditions in which there are conflicts between different perceptions, desires, or thoughts which lead to unpleasant emotional states **cognitive dissonances**.[7] We can even experience such cognitive dissonances as being physically unpleasant. Enduring them costs us strength and energy. That's why we want to get rid of them as quickly as possible.

People deal with cognitive dissonances (including those triggered by perceived differences in intercultural encounters) in different ways.[8] They often just deny the differences. Or they assume that others behave so differently on purpose. Some people react with a devaluation, i.e. regarding others as inferior. Aggression may also occur in such a case (sometimes even as far as attempting to 'destroy' the cause of the cognitive dissonance). These ways of dealing with cognitive dissonance are major causes of **discrimination** and **racism.**

Needless to say, none of these approaches lead to meaningful solutions in intercultural encounters.

Implications in an intercultural context

Culture

As we have seen, **we adopt the values, attitudes, and beliefs of the groups we live in**. This includes ways of thinking, problem solving, feeling, and acting, but also the group's language, religion, aesthetic ideas, traditions, customs, symbols, etc. We summarize this phenomenon with the word **culture.**

Geert Hofstede and his colleagues refer to culture as a **"collective programming of the mind"** or **"software of the mind."**[9] We share the same (or similar) culture with the people we live and grow up with, because we have learned it from them.

In this sense, culture is inherited. We learn it from our ancestors and pass it on to our descendants. Each generation adapts its culture to its respective living conditions, thus constantly developing it further.

A culture is neither 'right' nor 'wrong.' It is appropriate for the current circumstances of the group. People of a certain culture have learned to control their living environment in a particular way. In a completely different life situation, this kind of culture might no longer be appropriate. Likewise, another culture may not be appropriate for the specific life situation that a group is currently in.

Figure 2 People from different cultures see the world differently

Culture generally determines how we see the world. If you exchange ideas with someone from another culture about a different, third culture, you will realize that you notice different things about that third culture, and evaluate them in a different way (see Figure 2).

But culture also determines how we see ourselves, what we observe, and what meaning we give to what we observe.

Geert Hofstede, together with his son Gert Jan Hofstede, described **three levels at which we form our values, attitudes, and beliefs:**[10]

1. First, there is our common biological foundation as human beings. Here we have common, equal characteristics, which lie in our human nature. The biological foundation is universally the same for all people.

2. When we grow up in our families and closer groups, we learn their values, attitudes, and beliefs. These are shared by all members of that group and differ to a greater or lesser extent between different groups. Thus, they are essentially group-specific.

3. However, since we also have very individual experiences, we also develop values, attitudes, and beliefs that differ from those of our group. These are the very specific values, attitudes, and beliefs that are individual. They differ on a personal level.

Browaeys and Price distinguish between different levels of groups in which cultures develop.[11] Being born and brought up within certain groups, we develop our own individual culture. Depending on the groups we spend time with or live in, we develop corresponding 'shadows' of our individual culture:[12]

- We adopt a **professional culture** when we enter and pursue a particular profession. You may have noticed that people studying or working in other fields hold somewhat different values and views of the world than you do.

- If you then join a company, you will notice that it also has a specific **corporate culture**. The same applies to organizations, such as sports clubs or associations. In this case, we refer to an **organizational culture**.

- If you then look at the national level, you can also find overlaps between the people of one nation or country in their values, attitudes, and beliefs, which differ to a greater or lesser extent from those of people from other nations or countries. We then speak of **national culture**.

So when someone is talking about 'culture,' always ask yourself what level of culture is being referred to. Many studies about companies consider corporate or organizational culture. In this book, we will mainly deal with national culture and your own individual culture.

DIFFERENT LEVELS OF CULTURE

Meet with a person from a completely different profession to yours. Try to find out whether you have different views, set different priorities, and perhaps perceive things completely differently. This refers to the professional culture.

Compare the website of your own company or university with that of another company or university. What differences do you notice that could indicate different values or a different organizational culture, e.g. differences in contents, structure, colors, the way that readers are greeted, etc.?

Our individual culture is formed from the groups we have been a part of. The groups in which we currently live also contribute to our ongoing cultural development. They influence how we behave in each group, as we automatically adapt to some degree to the culture that prevails in the group. In this sense, we are fundamentally multicultural, as we belong to a number of groups (e.g. our family, a team at work or a class at school, a sports club, etc.) and each group has its own culture that influences us in a unique way.

YOUR MULTICULTURALISM—YOU AND YOUR GROUPS

Which groups do you belong to (e.g. family, university, company, sports club)?

- **Step 1:** Draw a circle that symbolizes you. Write your name inside the circle.
- **Step 2:** Draw additional circles for each of the groups you feel you belong to and label each one with a word that represents that group. Use the proximity of the circles to the one representing you to show how strongly or not you feel attached to the corresponding group. Draw lines to connect the circles that symbolize the groups with the circle that symbolizes you.
- **Step 3:** For each group, consider whether there are certain values, attitudes, and beliefs within the group that you consider to be characteristic of that group. Are there identifiers by which the group members recognize each other? How open is the group to accepting new members? How clearly does the group distinguish itself from other groups? Write key words which characterize the groups next to each circle.

Compare your notes on each group. Is there anything they have in common? To what extent do the values, attitudes, and beliefs of the groups match your own values, attitudes, and beliefs? Are there any clues as to why you are in these particular groups (and not in others)?

Don't worry if you have found it difficult to name your values, attitudes, and beliefs or those of your groups. It is not easy to identify which values, attitudes, and beliefs a culture follows.

(You can find a sample solution for this exercise on the companion website of this book at *www.econcise.com/CulturalSensitivityTraining*.)

In the field of cultural studies, one way of thinking about culture is like the cross-section of a lake.[13] On the surface of the lake, everything is clear and easy to see. Here we can observe everything well. There's a **material dimension** here (for example, clothing or symbols) as well as a **social dimension** (what is said, or how people behave). This is also the level that is often described as 'dos and don'ts' for how to behave in other countries.

When we dive a little deeper into the lake, the water gets murky. We can't see things that clearly any more. They become blurred, and sometimes ambiguous. We begin to interpret them through our own perceptions. This is where **norms, rules, and beliefs** come in. They are only partially visible.

If we dive even deeper to the bottom of the lake, we find things that have sunk into the mud. We can only guess about their meaning. This includes **what we assume, our values, feelings, and expectations**. We are often not even aware of them ourselves at a first glance. Some of them will always remain unconscious to us. This is called the '**mental dimension**.' It is this dimension that often causes difficulties in intercultural communication (we will come back to this point in Chapter 2 in connection with our ability to adapt to other cultures).

Discrimination and racism

There is nothing inherently 'wrong' with culture and cultural values. Even stereotypes have their justification to a certain extent, as we have seen above.

Potential difficulties can arise, however, in three different respects:

- If we **deny differences**, we may no longer interact with other people in an appropriate way. Communication and cooperation can fail.
- Something similar can happen **when stereotypical ideas are thoughtlessly transferred to all people of the corresponding group**. Again, individuals are no longer treated appropriately.
- Probably the most lasting negative effects occur when stereotypes are charged with a negative or sometimes even overly positive evaluation. We then speak of **prejudice**. This leads—in connection with power—to social discrimination and racism.

Social discrimination means that people are rejected or disadvantaged simply because they belong to a certain group. This can lead to negative behavior toward individuals or groups of people.

Many countries have laws that prohibit discrimination. While this might limit explicit discrimination, it often continues to exist in more subtle and implicit forms, including as a result of prejudiced laws and policies (institutional discrimination).

As we have seen, discrimination has its roots in **stereotyping**. Susan Fiske and her colleagues studied which stereotypes occur depending on the social status and competition that exists between groups:[14]

- They found **paternalistic stereotypes** for people whose status is lower, and with whom there is little competition. These are, for example, stereotypes toward old people, disabled people, or stay-at-home parents.
- They also found **admiring stereotypes**, for example, for celebrities and close allies, where their social status is high and there is little perceived competition with them.
- When competition is perceived, **disdainful stereotypes** exist toward people with low social status such as welfare recipients, unemployed people, refugees, or migrants.
- Toward people with high status and with whom there is also competition (such as rich people, technical experts, or successful Asian residents in the USA), Fiske et al. found **envious stereotypes.**

People usually sense quite precisely when they are being stereotyped by another person. If people feel that they are being evaluated by a negative image that someone else holds of them, they automatically try to hide certain characteristics that trigger this negative image. This influences, for example, how they behave (e.g. they might try to behave more 'properly'), which values they reveal, and how they present themselves.[15] Thus, stereotypically judged people cannot develop their true potential and fail to live a life that corresponds to their true selves.

YOUR OWN STEREOTYPES ACCORDING TO FISKE ET AL.

Try to conduct this exercise as objectively as possible. Be honest with yourself. Ideally, discuss your findings with someone else to reveal your own 'blind spots.'

Imagine four different people:

- An elderly or disabled person
- A celebrity
- A welfare recipient or migrant
- A fellow student who has better grades than you, or a colleague at work who earns significantly more money than you do

What characteristics do you attribute to these people? Write down the main ones. To what extent do these characteristics correspond to the stereotypes mentioned by Fiske et al.? Take into account your own position (e.g. as a privileged person, or an older person, or a migrant, etc.).

The next time you feel you are automatically judging a person according to this pattern, remind yourself that this is an automatic reaction and try to form a more nuanced picture of this person.

(You can find a template for this exercise on the companion website of this book at *www.econcise.com/CulturalSensitivityTraining*.)

While discrimination is primarily based on any characteristic (age, gender, social status, etc.), **racism** is a specific form of discrimination based on a person's belonging to a certain 'race'. In the case of racism, the stereotyping is based on easily recognizable characteristics such as skin color, eye shape, hair type, or language, although misjudgments very often occur. As with discrimination in general, there are both overt and covert forms of racism.

TEST YOUR OWN STEREOTYPES

Implicit Association Tests offer a way of testing your own stereotypes. Take an Implicit Association Test online to find out more about the stereotypes you hold, for example regarding age, gender or religion. At the time of writing, a free test was available at *https://implicit.harvard.edu/implicit/takeatest.html*.

Possible solutions for dealing with the automatisms

We've seen that our automatic reactions can cause a lot of problems, but it is possible to 'override' them by:

- spending as much time as possible in diverse environments,
- recognizing and interrupting the automatisms,
- practicing and automatizing new patterns of action, and
- developing social, emotional, and intercultural competence.

Let us now take a closer look at each of these strategies.

Immersing yourself in diverse environments

At the beginning of this chapter, we explored how the groups we live in shape our values, attitudes, and beliefs. The more diverse the people in these groups are, the more naturally we learn to deal with differences between people (and between ourselves and other people). Therefore, a **diverse environment** is the best training ground for intercultural competence.

Diversity can occur in very different ways. There are obvious characteristics such as age, gender, ethnicity, physical impairments, social class, and, maybe a little less obvious, sexual orientation and religion. Some characteristics are less visible at first sight, but we can find out about them, for example, through conversations. These include income, education, occupational background, location, family status, and parenthood. In Chapter 5 (on page 151), you will find an exercise that can help you make your contacts as diverse as possible.

In a diverse environment, you will typically recognize your automatisms more quickly because they are triggered again and again. You can also get quick feedback when you are unsure about others' reactions or your own. In a diverse environment, you can try out many of the things that we discuss in this book (especially the exercises). Such an environment will also constantly challenge you to find solutions that meet the different values, attitudes, and beliefs of as many people in that environment as possible.

You will typically also encounter a lot of different implicit, unconscious stereotypes of the highly diverse people in a diverse environment. You will often notice how people initially judge you based on their own stereotypes. Pay attention to how you feel about it.

At the same time, you will also perceive other people in the diverse environment through the filter of your own implicit stereotypes (at least when you first meet them). Do you notice how people react to these stereotypes? Doing so can prompt you to become aware when the stereotypes are occurring. From there, you can start to think about how you could avoid them.

A diverse environment can also make you realize that we usually perceive other groups as more homogeneous than they actually are. Perceiving differences within your own group or environment can help you realize that people within groups can actually be quite different. Thus you can train yourself to perceive people as individuals rather than as members of a group.

Last but not least, a diverse environment provides you with repeated opportunities to practice using **appreciative, non-discriminatory language**.

In order to make use of the learning opportunities that a diverse environment offers, you should reflect consciously on your experience and the outcomes of critical encounters as often as you can. Try to discuss your experience with other people (ideally from diverse backgrounds). This book offers some exercises for conscious reflection.

From fast thinking to slow thinking

Earlier in this chapter, we discussed the **continuum model of impression formation** by Fiske and Neuberg,[16] as well as the **model of fast and slow thinking** by Kahneman.[17] In doing so, we noted that our fast, efficient responses can lead to questionable decisions, miscategorization, and the hasty use of stereotypes.[18]

Kahneman lists a whole set of **heuristics** that we apply when we remain in the fast system of thinking.[19] These are 'rules of thumb' that either developed evolutionarily or that we have adopted from our parents and close relatives. These include simplifications, 'magic bullets,' and mental shortcuts, where we make decisions based on less information than we should because our fast system of thinking suggests that we already know enough. Through such simplifications, we can easily fall into the trap of not viewing people as they really are.

As human beings, however, we are free to pause for a moment before deciding or reacting (remember Viktor Frankl!). We are able to **step out of the fast system of thinking ('system 1') and switch to our slow system of thinking ('system 2')**. We can then start to think consciously, look for more information, and see people in their individuality rather than just pigeonholing them (see Figure 3).

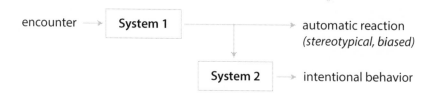

Figure 3 Switching from 'system 1' to 'system 2' thinking

Undoubtedly, it is difficult to break through the automatic processes of taking quick decisions and actions. At first, you will probably only retrospectively notice that you have once more judged and acted based on fast thinking. But the more often you realize this, the sooner you will be able to notice when you are about to act based on fast thinking. And once you consciously notice it, you will also be ready to switch from fast to slow thinking.

When you are working with your slow system of thinking and understand the possible ways of thinking about people and your interactions with them, you will be able to make informed decisions and act more appropriately in an intercultural context. This book will help you to achieve this.

Training your **conscious awareness** is the first step toward responding properly to intercultural encounters. Sometimes, however, when people notice that they are using their own stereotypes, they try to compensate in an exaggerated way.[20] We call this a **contrast effect**. Therefore, it makes sense to always get feedback on whether your efforts are producing adequate results.

Automatizing new ways of behaving

As we have already discussed, we perform many actions automatically (in the fast system of thinking).[21] We do not need to consciously think about these actions, and they do not cost us any cognitive power. That is also a reason why we fall back on these automatized actions again and again.

If we want to react with the slow system of thinking, it is costly for us. That's why we are often 'pushed back' into fast thinking. Exactly at this point, however, we have the potential to **interrupt the automated action**. Ideally, we are able to transfer the interruption of the fast reaction into an automatism, so it becomes second nature to interrupt our fast system of thinking. This is not easy to do, but it is possible.

Diverse environments, as discussed above, expose us again and again to stimuli to which we respond with fast thinking. At the same time, they also provide us with ample opportunities to practice different responses. We can train these responses again and again until they become a more or less unconscious habit for us. In clinical psychology, this is referred to as **habituation training**.[22]

Of course, we will never be able to completely unlearn our original, 'unconscious' responses. New habits will just override them. In stressful situations, when we need our cognitive powers for other things, we will likely fall back into our old automatized reaction patterns.

However, it's important to be aware that we do have a choice. Small steps that are repeated regularly are the key to success in acquiring new habits.[23] Maybe you want to train yourself to say "Stop!" and mentally press the pause button when you recognize that fast thinking is taking over. It probably won't be easy the first ten times, maybe not even the first fifty times, but the key is to keep trying again and again until it becomes a habit.

Fields of competence for intercultural interactions

Apart from the general ability to switch from fast to slow thinking, there are three fields of competence that you will need to develop for being able to effectively interact in an intercultural environment:

1. intercultural competencies,
2. social competencies, and
3. a general sensitivity and empathy to the other person.

Let us briefly take a look at these three fields of competence to conclude this chapter.

Intercultural competencies

Alexander Thomas provides a practice-oriented definition of intercultural competence. He **defines intercultural competence** as:

> *the ability to shape intercultural processes of action in such a way that solutions are found and misunderstandings are avoided or clarified so that the people involved can accept them.*[24]

The respective approaches to finding solutions may well differ from culture to culture. Intercultural competence is not seen as an aim in itself here, but as a way to find solutions and support the coexistence of people from different backgrounds.

Martin Cardel Gertsen suggested a general and widely used model of intercultural competence. It assumes that there are **three key aspects of intercultural competence** that influence each other:[25]

1. The **cognitive aspect**, which includes everything that we can grasp with our minds and our thinking. This includes knowledge about

cultures in general, but also knowledge about the 'dos' and 'don'ts' of certain cultures. This knowledge can be acquired quite well through reading.

2. The **behavioral aspect**, which includes our behavior when we interact with people from other cultures. How do we react to them? How do we respond to their reactions to us? How do we successfully shape interactions with people of other cultures? We can gain this type of knowledge in part by reading about how to behave meaningfully in intercultural interactions, and what our basic behavioral options are. But an even more important way of gaining behavioral intercultural competence is to try it out and experience it for ourselves—to actually interact.

3. The **affective (emotional) aspect** encompasses our inner feelings when we interact with people from other cultures. How do we feel in these situations? How do we feel when other people treat us differently than we expect? Can we control our own emotions in the process? This aspect also includes the ability to put ourselves in the other person's shoes. How does the other person feel when we treat them differently than they expected? Are we able to react appropriately to the other person's feelings?

We will return to this model in Chapter 5, when it comes to making a plan for developing your intercultural competencies to a higher level.

Social competencies

When Alexander Thomas once gave a lecture at our university, I asked him: "What is so special about intercultural competence? Isn't it simply general social competence?" He answered that of course, encounters with people from other cultures are encounters with people in general—and in encounters with other people, conflicts can always arise because (fortunately) people are different. Thomas called this a 'background noise.' He further argued that in encounters with people from other cultures, the particular difficulties that arise from the cross-cultural differences overlay this 'background noise,' meaning that the fluctuations of the 'background noise' are amplified.

This means that good social skills are definitely helpful for intercultural encounters. Conversely, however, **growing intercultural compe-**

tence also strengthens our social competence. You cannot separate one from the other. Everything you do for the development of your social competence will also help you with intercultural encounters. In this way, the advice in this book will also strengthen your social competence and help you in everyday life.

Sensitivity and empathy

Sensitivity and empathy are important aspects of (affective) intercultural competence. They are fundamental for being able to put yourself in another person's shoes, adopting different perspectives, observing and assessing your own behavior in interactions, and adapting your behavior to the situation. But it's also about recognizing what other people actually want to express with their actions and their words, and about recognizing how a person's individuality influences their actions.

Trying to understand what a person really wants to express will make it easier to achieve the desired outcomes or goals from an intercultural encounter.

The good old adage "When in Rome, act like a Roman" unfortunately does not help us much in intercultural situations.[26] It would mean putting one culture above another. It also raises the question of how 'Romans' really act. Someone who did not grow up in Rome would act like a Roman in light of their personal and cultural background. If 'non-Romans' imitate the behavior of a 'Roman,' they will likely do so without understanding or showing all the nuances of 'Roman' behavior. In addition, it would mean that if 'Romans' were to encounter 'non-Romans' in Rome, they would not adapt their behavior to their counterpart in any way. Whereas in reality, sensitivity and empathy for the other person play a decisive role in intercultural situations. It's a two-sided process.

Sensitivity and empathy can be gained through **frequent reflection** and especially **self-reflection**. This is what this book emphasizes. Besides acquiring some basic knowledge about cultures, we will look at ways to think about and interpret intercultural situations, our behavior in such situations, and the likely reasons for the behavior of the other person. There will be many exercises, too, to help you apply your new-found knowledge.

Let's get started!

So far we've introduced some of the basic concepts you need to understand how we all 'automatically' react when we meet people from other cultures. Let us now enter the world of intercultural encounters and explore how to best navigate within this world while still acting with authenticity.

KEY TAKEAWAYS FROM CHAPTER 1

1. Groups have an **evolutionary function**. We join different groups during our lifetime, and behave (at least to a certain degree) in conformity with the groups' norms and values.

2. The protection of one's own group was evolutionarily **important for survival**. We still prefer our own group to other groups.

3. **Stereotypes and categorizations** help us deal with the complexity of the world. They become a problem when they are associated with (especially negative) judgments, i.e. when they lead to prejudice.

4. Stereotypes are the outcome of **automatized reactions in our brain** (with 'system 1' thinking, our fast system of decision making).

5. We can **break the automatized reactions** and consciously choose to react differently (with 'system 2' thinking, our slow system of decision making).

6. **Sensitivity and empathy** are core elements of intercultural competence. We can acquire them through frequent interaction with people from other cultures and purposeful self-reflection. Experience and reflection build up competence.

Notes for Chapter 1

1   Frankl (2017).
2   Baumeister and Leary (1995).
3   Turner (1987).
4   Lipmann (2018).
5   Fiske and Neuberg (1990).
6   Kahneman (2012).
7   Festinger (1962).
8   Ibid.
9   Hofstede et al. (2010).
10 Hofstede and Hofstede (2006).
11 Browaeys and Price (2019).
12 Ibid.
13 Browaeys and Price (2019); Schneider and Barsoux (2003).
14 Fiske et al. (2002); Fiske (2018).
15 Yoshino and Smith (2013).
16 Fiske and Neuberg (1990).
17 Kahneman (2012).
18 Devine (1989).
19 Kahneman (2012).
20 Wegener and Petty (1997).
21 Kahneman (2012).
22 Felmingham et al. (2007).
23 Clear (2018).
24 Thomas (2003).
25 Gertsen (1990).
26 Weiss (1994).

2

Recognize: Cultural systems, cultural adaptability, and your own cultural profile

This chapter enables you to:

» Discover different ways of classifying cultural characteristics.
» Recognize the purpose and benefits of cultural classification systems and be aware of the limitations of such systems.
» Describe your own cultural background.

In the previous chapter, we saw that people are quite similar in their fundamental biological characteristics (e.g. their need for food, water, social contacts etc.) but differ in their values, attitudes, and beliefs, i.e. their culture. We have also observed that humans are often not very proficient in dealing with a lot of details in their external environment, and therefore like to classify things (and also people) with similar characteristics into categories.

Scientists build on this observation when they try to describe cultures and cultural differences with the help of **cultural classification systems** (or, in short, **cultural systems**). As scientists look at the world (and thus also at people) from different perspectives and with different research interests, different cultural systems have emerged, each with its particular area of application.

In this chapter, you will get an overview of a few of the best-known and most widely applied cultural classification systems. I will first introduce them to you and explain what they can be used for. In a few exercises, you can then create your own cultural profile based on these cultural systems.

These systems have many advantages, like helping us to quickly recognize important differences between certain cultures. But they also have their disadvantages. That's why we will take a look at the dangers of using cultural systems, too.

At the end of this chapter, we will take some additional aspects of your cultural background into account, and a final exercise will enable you to add further details to your cultural profile.

Cultural classification systems

What all classification systems have in common is the attempt to sort cultures according to how they answer questions about how we typically behave in certain aspects of our life.

Some questions are more connected to general everyday life, some relate to specific functions in companies, and others look at the values prevailing in a society. Depending on the type of answer to the respective question, a culture is assigned to a set of 'classes' or 'cultural dimensions.'

Most cultural systems are based on national cultures and focus on groups of people who have been growing up in the same country. For each group, they provide a 'typical' or 'usual' orientation of their thought patterns and behavioral tendencies. Keep in mind that this 'usual' orientation is not the same for everyone who is part of a particular group. Individuals can deviate from the 'usual' orientation to a certain degree. This entails some difficulties and poses potential dangers, which we will discuss at the end of this chapter.

You can use cultural systems to better understand your own cultural background. It does not matter which system you choose to work with. For a first attempt, I would recommend you try out a more general classification system. When you would like to analyze a concrete intercultural communication situation at a later stage, choose a more specific classification system or combine individual dimensions of different systems that cover the crucial aspects of the situation.

In order to give you a broad basis (a bit like a 'menu' that you can choose from), I will provide you with an overview of some of the best-known classification systems. For each system, I will also suggest where to find further information beyond the short overview provided in this book.

The cultural system according to Hofstede

Geert Hofstede's cultural system is one of the oldest, most widely used, and most hotly debated systems of classifying cultural differences.[1]

Hofstede conducted the first wave of data collection in the late 1960s and early 1970s in local subsidiaries of the global technology company IBM and included data from 70 different countries. The first four cultural dimensions were derived from 40 countries out of that original data set. A survey of students from 23 countries revealed a fifth cultural dimension ('long-term orientation') in 1985.

The sixth dimension (the 'indulgence' index) was added in a revision of the cultural system around 2010. With its six dimensions, Hofstede's cultural system tries to answer the question of how people think and act in different cultures in their **everyday life**.

Because the bulk of the empirical research was conducted in companies, this system is also often used in **management theories and practice**.

Hofstede's research is in itself a good example of how our cultural background influences our thoughts and actions. In his initial research, the Dutch researcher observed only four of the six dimensions that are being used today.

The two newer ones were only found when he collaborated with researchers from other countries: Michael Harris Bond (originally Canadian, but working in Hong Kong) and Michael Minkov (a Bulgarian). The new dimensions were more or less irrelevant in Hofstede's environment. He therefore had not included them in his surveys in the first place.

Hofstede's cultural system has repeatedly been **criticized** in various respects. This includes, for example, concerns that the model oversimplifies the complexities of cultures (a fate that is shared by most other cultural systems too), doubts about equating culture with nations (a recurring debate about the methodology of cultural research), and concerns that the system has become dated as the original research was carried out several decades ago.[2]

Hofstede has tried to deal constructively with some of the criticism. For example, there have been attempts to update the data on the cultural dimensions, and he has also explained that even if cultures do change, their relative ranking is not noticeably affected by these changes. Different studies have supported or refuted Hofstede's findings, depending on the perspective with which these studies were conducted.

Despite all the criticism, Hofstede's cultural system is still frequently used in both research and practice. We also use the system in this book, as it is easy to understand and covers a wide range of behavioral tendencies that affect our everyday life.

Each of the six dimensions of Hofstede's cultural system has two poles (with a value of 0 for the lower pole and 100 for the higher pole). The values are not percentages, but just a scale that shows how close or far a culture deviates from the two poles. The title of each dimension is designated according to the meaning of the higher pole, e.g. a high value of individualism means a tendency toward individualism, and a low value of individualism means a tendency toward collectivism. The same applies to the cultural dimension of masculinity: a high value of masculinity means a tendency toward masculinity, and a low value of masculinity means a tendency toward femininity.

High power distance versus low power distance (Power Distance Index, PDI)

The **power distance** dimension provides answers to the following questions:

- How do people in a certain culture deal with authorities and inequalities?
- How strong are the hierarchies that exist in a culture (e.g. in companies or society)?
- How far are differences in the distribution of power perceived and accepted?

A **high level of power distance** means that differences between people in terms of their social status, prestige, or wealth are expected or even desired. Children are expected to obey their parents, students await clear instructions from their teachers (and maybe also show a lower level of self-initiative), and subordinates are used to carrying out the instructions of their superiors. Superiors, in turn, are expected to act like kind, autocratic parents. Companies tend to be centrally organized and have strict hierarchies. Differences in salaries are large. Supervisors' offices are usually separate, often on the upper floor of the building. People strive for conformity.

According to Hofstede's classification, countries with high power distance include, for example, Malaysia, Russia, Venezuela, and India.

In societies with a **low level of power distance**, people are generally regarded as equal. Children have the same rights as adults. People meet each other 'at eye level.' Students are expected to take initiative and feel responsible for their learning. Employees are involved in decision-making processes. The ideal supervisor could be described as a 'creative democrat.' Companies are less hierarchical, and the role of hierarchies is mainly confined to facilitating work processes. Supervisors' offices typically do not look much different to employees' offices (and are often found on the same floor). People strive for independence.

Countries with low power distance include, for example, Austria, Israel, Sweden, and the Netherlands.

Individualism versus collectivism (Individualism Index, IDV)

The dimension of **individualism versus collectivism** answers the question of how independent or interdependent people are in a certain culture. In individualistic cultures, people are more oriented toward themselves (perceiving themselves as independent beings). In collectivist cultures, the 'we' becomes more important than the 'I,' as people feel integrated into and mutually dependent on a group. People tend to 'develop their personality' in individualistic societies, and adapt their personality to the group's values in collectivist societies.

This cultural dimension focuses on the relationships between people and the community. The way in which people live together in smaller or larger families is one expression of these relationships. The relationships between people and the community are also decisive for the values that people form and the behaviors they develop.

In countries with a **high individualism index**, people are expected to take care of themselves and their close (smaller) families. Growing up in such a country means learning to take and bear responsibility for yourself and your family. As a result, people develop a sense of 'I.' Identity is based on the individual. People in individualistic societies tend to say quite honestly and directly what they think, and they do not shy away from conflict. Moral standards are applied equally to all people in society. People are used to relying on their capabilities and following the official and implicit rules of the country on their career and development path. Good qualifications help in this process. Your job or your personal well-being is often seen as more important than your relationship with the group.

In companies, employees are freer to decide how to carry out their work. They build a calculating relationship with the company—it's all a balance of giving and taking. Professional experience is important.

People in individualistic societies enter friendships according to their individual preferences. They seek personal satisfaction.

Individualistic countries (those with a high individualism index) include many Western countries, for example, the USA, the Netherlands, France, and Poland.

In **collectivist countries** (those with a **low individualism index**), people have a strong sense of belonging to groups that take care of them but which also demand their loyalty in return. People grow up in larger groups and receive protection from them. They develop a sense of 'we' and form a group mentality. Identity is strongly based on the identity of the group to which they belong.

Within their groups, people in collectivist societies try to avoid conflicts. They strive for harmony in order to avoid harming the group. Moral standards may differ or can be applied differently from group to group.

People also consider the concerns of the group when making decisions about their career, and the group assists them in their career-related choices. The relationship with the group and its welfare are more important than the job and also more important than personal happiness.

A company is also considered as a group to which you develop a moral connection. It is really important to create and maintain good contacts within the group, and group decisions matter. Privacy refers to the whole group.

Countries with a low level of IDV (i.e. collectivist countries) include, many countries in Asia and South America (e.g. Indonesia, China, or Ecuador) and Ukraine.

Masculinity versus femininity (Masculinity Index, MAS)

The **masculinity versus femininity** dimension (measured with the MAS index) answers the basic question of whether we 'live to work' or 'work to live.' Do work-related goals like earning more and getting a promotion (in cultures with a high masculinity index), or personal goals like developing good relationships (in more 'feminine' cultures), take precedence when we make decisions? Is there a focus on 'being the best' (high MAS) or is it more important to do what you like (low MAS)?

In addition to the role of work in our lives, the masculinity versus femininity dimension is also about how social and cultural roles are distributed between men and women. This is where the possibly old-fashioned designation of this dimension comes from. Is there a clear separation of roles between men and women in a society (high MAS), or do women and men fill the same roles (low MAS)? This dimension is very critically discussed nowadays, because it is often connected exclusively with the equality of women and men, which was not the original intention.

In **countries with a high masculinity index**, competition, performance, and success are important factors. Whoever wins defines success. This system of achievement and success begins at school and permeates organizational and corporate life. Material success, a career, and achievement orientation are important objectives in 'masculine' societies. Money and things count a lot. What you do matters (more than who you are).

Feelings and emotions are seen as being more the preserve of women. Men are seen as being more oriented toward facts, implementation, and rigor. They are expected to show ambition. Superiors are decisive and assertive.

Challenges and individual decisions prevail in companies, but recognition and fairness play an important role, too. Conflicts are clearly named and dealt with directly. People live to work.

Countries with a relatively high MAS index, i.e. those which prefer to 'live to work,' include Japan, Venezuela, Germany, and South Africa.

In **countries with a low masculinity index,** values such as caring for each other, protecting other group members, and modesty dominate. In such countries, quality of life is a sign of success. Standing out from the crowd is not the primary goal. In these countries, we often find a strong welfare state. People and functioning relationships are important. Who you are is crucial—more than what you do.

Both men and women are considered as being sensitive and caring. It is fine for both genders to show feelings and emotions, too.

Supervisors can use their intuition, and they will also consider the opinions of employees in their decisions. Solidarity, cooperation, and group decision making prevail in companies. Conflicts are usually solved through consensus. People work to live.

Countries with a low MAS index, i.e. those which prefer to 'work to live,' include, for example, Angola, Bhutan, Denmark, Iceland, and Sweden.

High uncertainty avoidance versus low uncertainty avoidance (Uncertainty Avoidance Index, UAI)

The cultural dimension of uncertainty avoidance answers the question of to what extent uncertainty or instability is tolerated in a particular society.

The future is unknown in all cultures. But do we want to control it (high UAI) or can we just let it happen (low UAI)? The ambiguity of the future causes fears, and different cultures deal with these fears in different ways. Do people feel threatened by the unknown future (high UAI) or do they see opportunities in it (low UAI)? Has society created rules and taken safety precautions to deal with uncertainty (high UAI)? The answers to these questions differ between societies depending on their level of uncertainty avoidance.

In **societies with high uncertainty avoidance,** uncertainty is seen as dangerous and something that needs to be reduced or minimized. People permanently fight against the danger of uncertainty. They want to avoid unknown risks. There are many strict rules in such societies.

Time equals money in cultures with a high level of uncertainty avoidance. Business and stress seem to bring satisfaction. People tend to be less tolerant toward the thoughts and behaviors of others, which also means that foreigners can have quite a hard time in such countries. There are clear structures that should ideally not be changed. People tend to feel powerless in the face of external forces. Law and order have high priority.

There are also many written rules in companies. Employees decide in groups. Consensus is better than conflict. Competition and ambition are rare, and so is trust (as strict rules are preferred to trust). People tend to be loyal to their organization.

Countries with a high level of uncertainty avoidance include, for example, Greece, Malta, Belgium, and Peru.

In **societies with low uncertainty avoidance**, people are curious about the unknown. They take things as they come and respond with improvisation. Unknown risks are tolerated. People need fewer rules.

Time is not used as a means to structure the whole life, but provides a rather approximate orientation, and idleness brings satisfaction. In these countries, people largely avoid stress. They tolerate other thoughts and are open to new ideas and change in an atmosphere of diversity.

There are also fewer rules in companies. Employees make their own decisions. Conflicts can be constructive. There is competition and ambition, but also a high level of trust. In general, there is less loyalty to organizations than in countries with a high level of uncertainty avoidance.

Countries with low uncertainty avoidance include, for example, Jamaica, Vietnam, India, and Canada.

Long-term orientation versus short-term orientation (Long-Term Orientation Index, LTO)

The **long-term orientation** dimension answers the question of how people relate to the past, present, and future. Is it important for society to maintain a connection to the past (low LTO) or is it more concerned with the challenges of the present and future (high LTO)?

In **countries with a high level of long-term orientation**, the focus lies more on the future. People strive for a good education as the basis for their future. They expect success from sustained efforts and work consistently and patiently toward a goal. Decisions are based on traditions, experience, and the fulfillment of social obligations. Traditions are adapted to current requirements.

It is important for people to fulfill their duties to society at any cost. Frugality is a highly regarded value. A lot of money is spent on investing in the future. Resources are used carefully.

In more long-term-oriented societies, people have a clear social position. Relationships and networks are important. A 'rational approach' to problem solving prevails. People assume that the truth depends strongly on the situation, context, and time.

Countries with high LTO include, for example, South Korea, China, Russia, and Switzerland.

Since high levels of long-term orientation are predominantly found in East Asian countries—societies which have been strongly influenced by Confucianism—this cultural dimension is also sometimes referred to as 'Confucianism.'

In **countries with a low long-term orientation**, social changes are viewed with suspicion while time-honored traditions are preserved. Efforts and decisions should lead to results immediately (or at least in the short term). Although traditions are respected, immediate gains have an even higher priority.

Duties to society are fulfilled, but only within certain limits. Less money is invested into the future; you spend it when you earn it. Expenditures are often made only in response to social pressure.

In countries with low LTO levels, we find fewer relationships with ulterior motives. A person's status is not that important.

Another characteristic of countries with low long-term orientation is an 'analytical' approach to problem solving. People believe that there is an 'absolute truth,' and they want to find it.

Countries with low LTO include, for example, Nigeria, Iran, Australia, and Portugal.

Indulgence versus restraint (Indulgence Index, IND)

The cultural dimension of **indulgence versus restraint** answers the question of to what extent people try to control their desires and impulses. If you do not control your impulses and desires, it is called 'indulgence'; the opposite is called 'restraint.' People who live in societies with a high level of indulgence tend to live impulsively and fulfill their needs and desires quickly. A low level of IND means that it is more important to have your life 'under control' and to suppress your immediate desires in order to satisfy social moral standards.

In **'restrained' societies**, people self-regulate their behavior and have their impulses under control. They tend to be pessimistic, cynical, reserved, and self-controlled. There's also a stronger sense of injustice.

Status is more important than functionality (what you contribute to society). Good work is rewarded with material things (which is why houses or cars are particularly important in such societies). In contrast, friends and leisure time are less important.

By regulating themselves through strict social norms, people suppress the satisfaction of their needs. There are clear (albeit partly implicit) social rules about when and how it is appropriate to indulge in certain kinds of needs.

Countries with low IND levels, i.e. 'restrained' societies, include Pakistan, Albania, Romania, and Serbia.

In **'indulgent' societies**, people follow their impulses much more than in 'restrained' ones. They tend to be optimistic, happy, extroverted, and live in the present.

Functionality is more important than status. Material things are less important than, for example, friends and leisure time. People indulge relatively freely in the satisfaction of basic and natural human desires linked to vitality and fun.

Countries with a high level of indulgence include, for example, Angola, New Zealand, the United Kingdom, and Canada.

YOUR OWN CULTURE ACCORDING TO HOFSTEDE'S CULTURAL SYSTEM

In this exercise, you will take a look at your own cultural background using Hofstede's cultural system.

- **Step 1:** Draw six horizontal lines and label them with the name of the low pole of the Hofstede dimension on the left and the name of the high pole of the Hofstede dimension on the right, e.g. collectivism on the left and individualism on the right. Label the left side of each line with 0 and the right side with 100.
- **Step 2:** Read the descriptions of the dimensions above, and try to objectively and calmly consider to what extent they apply to you. You will notice that it is not easy to come to a clear conclusion since you will lean toward the low pole with some aspects and toward the high pole with others. Try to locate a midpoint between these extremes that you feel best represents you. Put a point on the line that belongs to this dimension, at the place where you see yourself located in this particular dimension.
- **Step 3:** Finally, you can connect the points with lines and get your cultural profile according to Hofstede. If you return to this exercise and feel that your choices could be refined, simply change them.

Please keep this profile. We will continue to work with it in the following exercises and chapters. You can also supplement it with the dimensions of the cultural systems described below.

The following article includes a questionnaire that measures the first five cultural dimensions according to Hofstede on an individual level:

Yoo, B., Donthu, N., & Lenartowicz, T. (2011). Measuring Hofstede's five dimensions of cultural values at the individual level: Development and validation of CVSCALE. *Journal of International Consumer Marketing, 23*(3–4), 193–210.

If you want to, find out which values this questionnaire determines for you. (Note that the questionnaire used by Hofstede himself, found in his book *Culture's Consequences*, is only applicable to the country or group level, not individuals.)

···

More information about the Hofstede model

Check out the following weblinks (which were available at the time of writing) and literature if you are interested in more detailed information about the Hofstede model:

- *https://www.hofstede-insights.com/product/compare-countries/*
- *https://www.map-consult.com/en/hofstede-model.html*
- Hofstede, G. (2001). *Culture's Consequences: Comparing Values, Behaviors, Institutions, and Organizations Across Nations*, 2nd ed. Thousand Oaks, CA: Sage Publications.
- Hofstede, G., Hofstede, G. J., & Minkov, M. (2010). *Cultures and Organizations: Software of the Mind: Intercultural Cooperation and its Importance for Survival*, 3rd ed. New York, NY: McGraw Hill.

···

The cultural system according to Schwartz

Shalom Schwartz's cultural system is strongly theory-based and has sociological and psychological roots.[3] These roots lie primarily in the concept of values in sociology and the concepts of motivation and needs in psychology.

This system is also used in the **World Values Survey**, an international study that was conducted in 22 different countries for the first time in 1981,[4] and has since been followed by five more survey waves. Every two years since 2002, a similar survey has also been published only for European countries (**European Values Study**). This survey is also based on Schwartz's system.

Schwartz is interested in the importance of goals that people in different countries pursue, and derives **values** from them. These values are not completely independent but influence each other. Cultures are therefore classified according to the values (and attitudes that are derived from these values) that prevail in certain societies.

Although we cannot directly infer actions from the prevailing values, internalized values help people to choose between alternatives, resolve conflicts, and make decisions.

The ten cultural dimensions (or values) according to Schwartz are:[5]

- **Self-direction:** this value is based on the need to feel in control, autonomy, and independence. It's about thinking and acting independently. This includes, for example, setting your own goals, curiosity, creativity, and freedom.
- **Stimulation:** this value is based on the need for variety. It's about always seeking new challenges in your life and it's also related to a certain level of excitement. This includes, for example, an exciting, varied life, as well as daring to do something different.
- **Hedonism:** this value is based on the need for pleasure and fulfillment. It is all about sensual satisfaction. This includes, for example, enjoying life and a certain degree of licentiousness.
- **Achievement:** this value is based on the need to achieve personal success and demonstrate competencies according to social standards. It is about the achievement of goals. Ambition, success, influence, and intelligence are particularly important in societies with a high level of achievement orientation.
- **Power:** this value is based on the need to have prestige and social status, dominate other people, and have resources at your command. It's about how you generally display yourself in society. This includes, for example, authority, social power, and wealth.
- **Security:** this value is based on the need for safety, harmony, and stability in society and in your personal and societal relationships. It's not only about security at the individual level, but also about the security of society as a whole. The security value therefore also includes, for example, an appreciation of social order, family security, national security, and the feeling of belonging.
- **Conformity:** this value is based on the need to restrain actions and impulses that might violate social expectations or norms. It involves

suppressing desires and inclinations that might otherwise harm the community. The expectations that people need to comply with may change according to the current situation. People conform to expectations in order to avoid negative consequences. This value includes, for example, self-discipline, politeness, and obedience.

- **Tradition:** this value is based on the need to express experiences and stories that are shared by the community in the form of rites, beliefs, and norms of behavior. It's about group solidarity, shared values, religion, and cultural customs. These rules are located in the past and do not change (or change only very slowly). The value of tradition includes, for example, acceptance of your own contribution to life, modesty, and piety.

- **Benevolence:** this value is based on the need to be part of a well-functioning group and to belong. It's about maintaining and improving the well-being of your own group and voluntarily caring for the well-being of others. The desire to care for the group comes from within. It includes honesty, forgiveness, responsibility, loyalty, true friendship, and meaning in life.

- **Universalism:** this value is based on the need to survive both as an individual and as a group. It's about understanding, appreciation, and tolerance for all people and for nature. It includes, for example, open-mindedness, equality, wisdom, and inner harmony.

EXERCISE

YOUR OWN CULTURE ACCORDING TO THE CULTURAL SYSTEM OF SCHWARTZ

This exercise can be used as a supplement to the last exercise, so you can continue your notes from there.

- **Step 1:** Draw ten horizontal lines and label them with the ten values according to Schwartz. Label the left side of each line as 'low value' and the right side as 'high value.'

- **Step 2:** Carefully read the descriptions of the values, and consider how important these values are to you personally and how you would prioritize them in comparison to other values. This is not an easy task, because we often have contradictory feelings about the relative importance of certain values. Try to find a ranking for each one that feels 'right' for you. Use a point to mark on each line how much weight you ascribe to each value.
- **Step 3:** Finally, connect the points with lines and get your cultural profile according to Schwartz. If you return to this exercise and feel that your choices could be refined, simply change them.

Please keep this profile too. We will continue to work with it in the following exercises. You can also supplement it with the dimensions of the cultural systems described below.

There are two questionnaires that you can use to determine your priorities for the Schwartz values: the Schwartz Value Survey and the Portrait Values Questionnaire.[6] Since the **Portrait Values Questionnaire** asks rather culture-independent questions, I would recommend you use this one. At the time of writing you can find a reliable version here: *https://doi.org/10.6102/zis234*. You have to register for free at gesis (Leibnitz Institut für Sozialwissenschaften). The questionnaire is available in English and many other languages.

· ·

More information about the Schwartz model

Check out the following weblinks (which were available at the time of writing) and literature if you are interested in more detailed information about the Schwartz model:

- *https://europeanvaluesstudy.eu/*
- *https://www.europeansocialsurvey.org/*
- *https://irfankhawajaphilosopher.com/2015/08/12/the-schwartz-theory-of-basic-values-and-some-implications-for-political-philosophy/*
- *https://i2insights.org/2022/05/10/schwartz-theory-of-basic-values/*
- Schwartz, S. H. (2012). An overview of the Schwartz theory of basic values. *Online Readings in Psychology and Culture, 2*(1).

· ·

COMPARISON OF THE CULTURAL SYSTEMS OF HOFSTEDE AND SCHWARTZ

As you have worked through the last two exercises, you may have noticed that the two cultural systems use different aspects to describe culture. Hofstede looks more at people's actions, whereas Schwartz asks about the motives that lead people to act in specific ways.

Think about which perspective is more appropriate for which type of intercultural situation.

The cultural dimensions of the GLOBE project

The **GLOBE project**[7] started in the early 2000s. It was originally focused on **cultural practices** and **differences in leadership styles** between countries. In the meantime, however, it has also become more concerned with issues of general and interpersonal trust.

Unlike other cultural systems, the GLOBE project asks about both **how culture *is* practiced** and **how it *should* be practiced**. It also considers the character traits of effective leaders. Large-scale surveys were conducted in 2004 and 2014, with additional data being gathered in 2020. The survey results were used to create regional clusters of countries with similar cultural characteristics.

The GLOBE project survey includes nine cultural dimensions and **six global leadership dimensions**: charismatic/value-based, team-oriented, participative, humane-oriented, autonomous, and self-protective.

Since the **cultural dimensions in the GLOBE project** have a lot of overlap with Hofstede's dimensions, I will only give brief descriptions of them here. The dimensions are measured on a scale from 1 (low proficiency) to 7 (high proficiency):

- **Performance orientation** describes the extent to which a group encourages and rewards its members to improve their performance and achieve excellence.

- **Assertiveness** describes the extent to which it is accepted that people are assertive, confrontational, and aggressive in following their interests.
- **Future orientation** describes the extent to which people are oriented toward the future, and includes, for example, planning, directing investments toward the future, and deferring rewards.
- **Humane orientation** describes the extent to which people behave fairly, altruistically, generously, and caringly toward others and are rewarded for such behavior by the group.
- **Institutional collectivism** describes the extent to which institutional practices are designed to collectively decide how to distribute resources and promote collective action.
- **In-group collectivism** describes the extent to which people enjoy living in their organizations and families, are loyal to them, and are proud of cohesion.
- **Gender egalitarianism** describes the extent to which genders are perceived as being equal.
- **Power distance** describes the extent to which people accept differences in status and power as normal and good.
- **Uncertainty avoidance** describes the extent to which people want to reduce the unpredictability of the future, and rely on social norms, rules, and procedures.

EXERCISE

YOUR OWN CULTURE ACCORDING TO THE GLOBE PROJECT

As you will have noticed, there is quite a lot of overlap between Hofstede's cultural system and that of the GLOBE project. However, there are also differences, so it is worth evaluating your own culture using both systems. You can continue adding to your notes from the previous exercises.

- **Step 1:** Draw nine horizontal lines and label them with the nine dimensions of the GLOBE project. Label the left side of each line with the value '1' (low) and the right side with '7' (high).
- **Step 2:** Carefully read the descriptions of the dimensions above, and think about how much each one applies to you. Place a point on each line where you see yourself in these dimensions.
- **Step 3:** Finally, you can connect the points again to get your cultural profile according to the GLOBE project. If you return to this exercise and feel that your choices could be refined, simply change them.

Please keep this profile. We will continue to work with it in the following exercises. You can also supplement it with the dimensions of the cultural systems described below.

If you would like to determine your GLOBE values with the help of a questionnaire, you can use the one available on the GLOBE Project website (at the time of writing, *https://globeproject.com/data/GLOBE-Phase-2-Beta-Questionnaire-2006.pdf*).

··

More information about the GLOBE project

Check out the following weblink (which was available at the time of writing) and literature if you are interested in more detailed information about the GLOBE study:

- *https://globeproject.com*
- Chhokar, J. S., Brodbeck, F. C., & House, R. J. (eds) (2019). *Culture and Leadership Across the World: The GLOBE Book of In-Depth Studies of 25 Societies*. Hove: Psychology Press.
- House, R. J., Dorfman, P. W., Javidan, M., Hanges, P. J., & Sully De Luque, M. F. (2013). *Strategic Leadership Across Cultures: The GLOBE Study of CEO Leadership Behavior and Effectiveness in 24 Countries*. Thousand Oaks, CA: Sage Publications.

··

Other cultural systems

In addition to the well-known and widely used cultural dimensions of Hofstede, Schwartz, and the GLOBE project, there are many other cultural systems, too. Many of them are very specific, containing only a few dimensions or sometimes even just one dimension.

Since some of these alternative models can be very helpful for the interpretation of specific communication situations, I would like to give you a quick overview of a few salient ones.

The cultural system of Kluckhohn and Strodtbeck

Like Hofstede, Kluckhohn and Strodtbeck are concerned with looking at how people answer basic questions about everyday life.[8] For each question they provide two completely opposing answers as well as a more neutral one that covers the middle ground. Thus, for every question, each culture can be classified into one out of three groups:[9]

- The first question is about the **character of human nature**. It can be *good* or *evil* or a *mixture of good and evil*.
- The second question is about the **relationship of humans to nature**. The two extreme positions are that either *humans dominate nature* or *nature dominates humans*. Kluckhohn and Strodtbeck consider *harmony between humans and nature* as the middle value.
- The third question is about the **time period that people are focused on**. *Past* and *future* are the two extremes. The *present* is the neutral answer.
- The fourth question is about the **goals that people pursue with their activities**. People can *spontaneously express their needs* and do everything for their immediate satisfaction. On the other end of the spectrum, *people purposefully try to achieve measurable goals*. Kluckhohn and Strodtbeck see *comprehensive development of the self* as the neutral position.
- The fifth question examines the **relationship between people**. People can place themselves in *hierarchies*. But they can also *live individualistically on their own*. These are the two extreme positions. *People living together collectivistically* is seen as the neutral position.

YOUR OWN CULTURE ACCORDING TO KLUCKHOHN AND STRODTBECK

- **Step 1:** Add five more horizontal lines to your notes from the previous exercises and label them so it's clear which question in the Kluckhohn and Strodtbeck model each line is representing. Label the left side of each line so you can see that it belongs to one extreme, and label the right side of the line with the other extreme. Mark the middle of each line as the 'neutral' position.
- **Step 2:** Consider each of the questions above and think about whether you lean toward one of the extremes or toward the neutral position. Use a point to mark your position for each question.
- **Step 3:** Finally, connect the points with lines to get your cultural profile according to Kluckhohn and Strodtbeck. If you return to this exercise and feel that your choices could be refined, simply change them.

   Please keep this profile. We will continue to work with it in the following exercises. You can also supplement it with the dimensions of the cultural systems described below.

....

More information about the Kluckhohn and Strodtbeck cultural system

Check out the following literature if you are interested in more detailed information about the Kluckhohn and Strodtbeck system:

- Kluckhohn, F. R., & Strodtbeck, F. L. (1961). *Variations in Value Orientations*. Evanston, IL: Row, Peterson.

....

The cultural system of Trompenaars and Hampden-Turner

Trompenaars and Hampden-Turner focus primarily on **everyday and business life**.[10] For over ten years, beginning in the 1990s, they surveyed around 15,000 managers in 28 countries and derived seven cultural dimensions from their study.

The cultural dimensions are related to different aspects of the business world. Each dimension has two extremes.

Five of the Trompenaars and Hampden-Turner dimensions look at different aspects of **relationships between people**, one dimension represents the **relationship of people to time**, and another dimension represents the **relationship of people to the environment**.

Here is a short overview of the seven dimensions:[11]

- **Obligation** comprises the two poles *universalism* and *particularism*. Do people care more about rules or about their relationships? In universalistic societies, rules and norms apply equally to all people. In particularistic societies, norms and rules depend on specific group affiliations.
- **Relationships with people** comprises the two poles *individualism* and *collectivism*. Do people focus on their own interests or on the well-being of the group? This dimension is comparable to Hofstede's individualism dimension.
- **Emotional orientation** comprises the two poles *neutral* and *affective*. Can people uncover feelings and emotions? In neutral societies, people control and 'master' their feelings and emotions, whereas in affective societies, they reveal emotions, enjoy physical contact, and find silence uncomfortable.
- **Structuring** comprises the poles *specific* and *diffuse*. Are different areas of life interwoven or is there a clear separation, for example, between work and private life? Also, texts and conversations can be either more structured or more diffuse.
- **Legitimating power and status** comprises the poles *achievement* and *ascription*. Do people attain a certain position through their own achievement or are they born into their position? In achievement-oriented societies, people have to work for their place in life, and performance criteria play a role, for example, in the allocation

of jobs. In ascription-oriented societies, your origin (e.g. your family background), title, and seniority are more important than achievements, and status symbols play a major role.

- **Time** comprises the poles *sequential* and *synchronous*. Are people completing one task after another or do they deal with several things at the same time? In sequential societies, punctuality and precise timing are important. People typically do one thing at a time. In synchronous societies, the present is especially important. People are used to doing several things at once.
- **Relationship to the environment** comprises the poles *inner-directed* and *outer-directed*. The central question is whether you can control the environment or whether you are at the mercy of external influences. In inner-directed societies, people assume they can influence events (and therefore often question them). In outer-directed societies, people assume that they cannot influence external events (and are therefore more willing to just accept them).

EXERCISE

YOUR OWN CULTURE ACCORDING TO TROMPENAARS AND HAMPDEN-TURNER

- **Step 1:** Add seven more horizontal lines to your notes from the last exercises and label them with the names of the dimensions from the Trompenaars and Hampden-Turner system. Label the left side of each line with the name of one pole and the right side with the name of the other pole.
- **Step 2:** Carefully read the descriptions of the dimensions above, and think about which poles you lean toward. Place a point on each line where you see yourself in this dimension.
- **Step 3:** Finally, you can connect the points with lines to get your Trompenaars and Hampden-Turner cultural profile. If you return to this exercise and feel that your choices could be refined, simply change them.

> Please keep this profile. We will continue to work with it in the fol-
> lowing exercises. You can also supplement it with the dimensions of the
> cultural systems described below.

....

More information about the cultural system according to Trompenaars and Hampden-Turner

Check out the following literature if you are interested in more detailed information about the Trompenaars and Hampden-Turner system:

- Trompenaars, F., & Hampden-Turner, C. (1998). *Riding the Waves of Culture: Understanding Cultural Diversity in Global Business*, 2nd ed. New York, NY: McGraw Hill.

....

The cultural dimensions of Hall

Hall's cultural dimensions refer to **differences in communication behavior**.[12] They are mainly derived from episodic examples, which means that Hall observed communication situations in different countries and tried to find similarities and differences in the behavior of the communication partners. Each of the dimensions has two extremes. The placement of the countries results from how strongly they lean toward one or the other extreme.

I will outline the three most important dimensions here. The other three dimensions (information flow, action chains, and interface formation) are derived from these **three 'basic' dimensions**, and will therefore not be discussed in this book:

- **Context** comprises the poles *high context* and *low context*. The key question here is how much accompanying information people need when they talk to each other. In low-context societies, only the spoken words and the conveyed facts count. In high-context societies, a lot of additional information lies in facial expressions, gestures, or general knowledge that provides background information to the conversation.

- **Space** comprises the poles *private* and *public*. In this dimension, space means everything that is around us, starting with the space next to our skin. The more a society tends toward public space (when private space is smaller), the more tolerable it is for people to get close to each other. In societies with an orientation toward public space, it is more common for people to use other people's things, for example, or to sit down at another person's desk in an office. In societies with an orientation toward private space, on the other hand, people keep a greater distance from each other and avoid sharing their private things with one another.
- **Time** comprises the poles *monochronic* and *polychronic*. It is quite similar to Trompenaars and Hampden-Turner's dimension of 'time.' In monochronic societies, events proceed one after the other. People value strict timing and punctuality, establish short-term relationships with each other, speak relatively slowly, and plan for the long term. In polychronic societies, multiple events occur simultaneously. People are flexible with time, frequently switch between different jobs, often form lifelong relationships with each other, speak relatively quickly, and tend to plan only for the short term.

EXERCISE

YOUR OWN CULTURE ACCORDING TO HALL

- **Step 1:** Add three more horizontal lines to your notes from the previous exercises and label them with the names of the dimensions from Hall's cultural system. Label the left side of each line with the name of one pole and the right side with the name of the other pole.
- **Step 2:** Carefully read the descriptions of the dimensions above, and think about which poles you lean toward. Place a point on each line where you see yourself in this dimension.

- **Step 3:** Finally, you can connect the points with lines to get your cultural profile. If you return to this exercise and feel that your choices could be refined, simply change them.

  Please keep this profile. We will continue to work with it in the following exercises. You can also supplement it with the dimensions of the cultural system described below.

....

More information about Hall's cultural system

Check out the following books if you are interested in more detailed information about Hall's system:

- Hall, E. T. (1973). *The Silent Language: An Anthropologist Reveals How We Communicate by Our Manners and Behavior*. New York, NY: Doubleday.
- Hall, E. T. (1977). *Beyond Culture*. New York, NY: Anchor Books.
- Hall, E. T. (1982). *The Hidden Dimension*. New York, NY: Doubleday.
- Hall, E. T., & Hall, M. R. (1990). *Understanding Cultural Differences*. Boston, MA: Intercultural Press.

....

The cultural system of Lewis

Richard Lewis is an English communications consultant. His cultural model looks at societies, particularly in terms of their **communication habits**.[13] Based on 150,000 responses to an online questionnaire from 68 different countries, Lewis divides countries into three rough groups. There is one dimension with three manifestations in his cultural system. Lewis depicts these three manifestations as the three corners of a triangle, and arranges the countries on the sides of that triangle according to how strongly they are associated with one corner or the other on the respective side of the triangle.

Linear-active societies resemble societies with monochronic time orientation (more or less comparable to Hall). People like to plan, schedule, and organize, as well as complete one task at a time. They do not interrupt each other in conversations, are polite, and turn toward each other when talking. They suppress their feelings now and then, and are very 'matter of fact' when dealing with problems.

Multi-active societies resemble societies with a polychronic time orientation (more or less comparable to Hall). People are communicative and people-oriented, and tend to work on different tasks simultaneously. They interrupt each other in conversations, are emotional, and prioritize people and feelings over pure facts. Relationships have higher priorities than schedules. Truth is context-dependent.

In **reactive societies**, it's all about saving face. People are polite, indirect, pay respect to each other, and make decisions in a relatively unemotional way. They act according to basic principles, and give equal weight to people and facts when problems arise.

EXERCISE

YOUR OWN CULTURE ACCORDING TO LEWIS

- **Step 1:** Draw an equilateral triangle (adding to your notes from the previous exercises) and label the three corners with the three types of society in Lewis' cultural system (linear-active, multi-active, and reactive).
- **Step 2:** Carefully read through the descriptions of the societies above and think about which two of them you lean toward. Pick the corresponding side of the triangle. Now think about where you feel you sit between these two societies. Place a point on that side of the triangle so that it represents your position between the two societies. If you return to this exercise and feel that your choices could be refined, simply change them.

    Please keep this profile. We will continue to work with it in the following exercises. You can also supplement it with other cultural systems not described in this book if you like.

More information Lewis' cultural system

Check out the following book if you are interested in more detailed information about Lewis' system:

- Lewis, R. D. (2018). *When Cultures Collide: Leading Across Cultures*, 4th ed. London: Nicholas Brealey Publishing.

Be cautious when using cultural systems

Cultural systems can be very helpful. But remember that they are just **models**. Models never fully represent reality. They are created for a specific purpose and leave out many details. That is why it is important to consider the functional purpose of each cultural system (see Figure 4 for an overview), what they can be used for, and what they are not suitable for.

	Society	Everyday life	Business	Communication
Hofstede		●	●	
Schwartz	●	●		
GLOBE			●	
Kluckhohn & Strodtbeck		●		
Trompenaars & Hampden-Turner		●	●	
Hall				●
Lewis				●

Figure 4 Cultural systems and their main purpose

When we apply cultural systems, it means that we **categorize people into groups that we assume have the 'same' culture**. We try to describe this group with certain values and behaviors. So far, so good—but we need to be aware that **within these groups of people, people can strongly differ from each other**. Therefore, we cannot say that "all people in this group share the same values or exhibit the same behavior."

The classifications, numbers, or relative positions that countries are assigned to in the cultural systems do not refer to a single person. They are an **average value** for all the people in a particular group and are only valid for the group *as a whole*. You will have a hard time, for example, in trying to find an Indian who corresponds to all the values of India according to Hofstede.

You may wonder why these cultural systems exist at all, then. Well, they can give us a **rough orientation** when we meet people of a certain culture for the first time. We can prepare ourselves for what we can expect in principle in a particular country.

It is not possible, however, to derive from the dimensions the concrete values and behavior of a particular person. We can only assume that a person from that culture is likely to act in a way that is in line with their country's cultural tendency. It is still possible (and not very uncommon), however, that this person differs from what we imagine about a culture based on its position in a cultural system.

EXERCISE

THE DISTRIBUTION OF CULTURAL CHARACTERISTICS WITHIN AND BETWEEN CULTURES

Construct a graph with both the X and Y axes starting at 0 (or use the template on the companion website of this book at *www.econcise.com/ CulturalSensitivityTraining*). Draw a bell curve on the X-axis of your graph. The X-axis represents the values for any cultural dimension on a scale of 0 to 100. The line of the bell curve illustrates how many people in one particular country adhere to or exhibit that dimension.

Draw a vertical line through the apex of the bell curve. It will intersect the X-axis to indicate where this particular country sits in this cultural dimension. For example, if we pretend the bell curve represents the individualism index for your home country, you can see that most people in your home country have an individualism index that is close to the mean value for your home country (i.e. the value of the individualism index for your home country as a whole). The further the index value is away from the mean, the fewer people in your home country match the individualism index value for your home country as a whole. But there are still quite a few of those outliers, as the index value can vary considerably within a country. Compare your drawing with Figure 5.

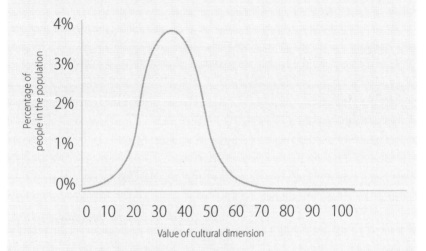

Figure 5 Distribution of dimension values in a country

Now let's conduct another thought experiment. Draw another bell curve on the graph that overlaps the first one. This bell curve represents a different country. The overlap means that there are people from different countries who share the same cultural values. But as you can see, there are only a few of them. If you imagine shifting the second bell curve to the left or right, you will see that the area of overlap becomes larger as the two curves approach each other and smaller as you move them further apart. This is called **'cultural distance.'**

You can see that the further apart the cultures are from each other, the fewer people share the same values. In contrast, the closer the cultures, the more people share the same values. Compare your drawing with Figure 6.

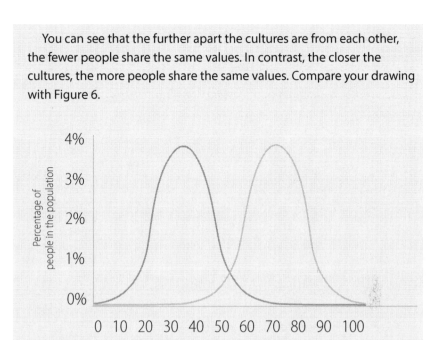

Figure 6 Overlapping of dimension values between two national cultures

When applying cultural systems, pay attention to the groups of people for which these systems were set up. The systems I have presented in this chapter apply to countries. However, cultural systems can also apply to companies (we then speak of corporate culture) or social groups within certain societies (also called milieus).

When choosing a cultural system for your research work, you might consider two further points:

- The researchers who developed these cultural systems conducted questionnaires or observed people at work, and then derived the dimensions or values of their systems from that research. Before you start working with one system, therefore, inform yourself about how many countries and **how many people within particular countries the researchers included in their study**. This information is important for you to be able to assess how reliable the cultural systems are (especially for particular countries).

- Some cultural systems do not provide **numerical values** for their dimensions. You therefore cannot use these systems for quantitative studies.

In this book, we use the cultural systems primarily to **help us think about our own cultural background**, i.e. as an inspiration for thinking about ourselves. We don't need concrete numbers to do this, as a rough orientation is sufficient for that purpose.

The adaptability of one's culture

When looking at cultural systems, you might come to think that once you hold certain cultural values, they remain fixed for your whole life. However, if you remember our discussion in Chapter 1 about how we acquire our cultural values, you might have already suspected that **cultural values can also change and evolve**. We can even actively try to change our values (otherwise, a book like this one would be completely pointless).

With the following exercise, let us imagine to what extent such a change of cultural values can be possible in principle.

EXERCISE

HOW ADAPTABLE ARE YOUR CULTURAL VALUES?

Take another look at your graph with the bell curves from the last exercise (or recreate Figure 6 in your notes).

Draw a vertical line at any point on the graph: this represents you and your individual cultural value. Now place two further vertical lines to the left and right of your individual cultural value line. It is best to use a different color here. You can also hatch the area between these two lines. This is the area in which you will be able to adjust your own culture. The width of the area shows the extent to which you can adapt your culture.

Increasing the range of your adaptability is the purpose of intercultural training. Compare your drawing with Figure 7.

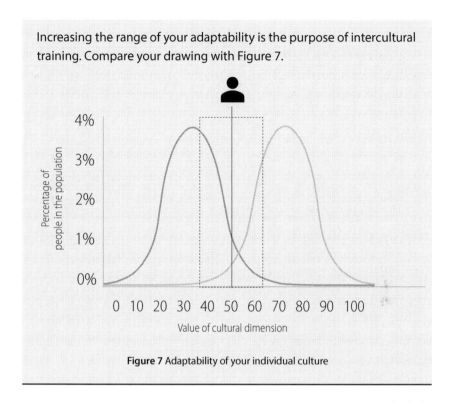

Figure 7 Adaptability of your individual culture

The extent to which you will be able to adapt your cultural values will (besides other factors like your interest in and prior knowledge about the other culture) depend on the **visibility of cultural characteristics** (remember the 'lake' metaphor on page 16 in Chapter 1).

It is relatively easy to dress according to another culture, to eat the food of another culture, or to celebrate the festivals and rituals of another culture. If you want to behave according to the rules and customs of another culture, it may take some effort, but eventually, you will succeed.

Adaptation becomes relatively difficult, however, when it comes to the **implicit values** of another culture (e.g. the importance of family ties, tacit expectations of other people's behaviors, or the deeper meaning of certain terms). In this case, you have to consciously adapt your own values and behavior. It's about getting to know other people's perspectives and trying to see the world through their eyes rather than through your own. You will need some tools to help you with that kind of adjustment.

If you would like to increase your range of adaptation, it is necessary to learn how to adopt other people's perspectives. Much cross-cultural training addresses the visible aspects of another culture, or those that are easy to learn. Few address the implicit values and behaviors. The next two chapters will help you adapt (at least to some extent) to the implicit characteristics of a culture, too.

You will notice that there are cultures that you like more and others that you like less. Don't be discouraged by this! Start by trying to adapt to the cultures you enjoy more. The lessons learned from this will help you when you have to deal with a culture you might not like so much at first sight.

Your cultural repository (or 'overall cultural profile')

I would like to offer you one last thought for this chapter, which summarizes and applies some of the concepts that we have discussed. It is the idea of creating your own **cultural repository** (or '**overall cultural profile**').

You may have heard the term 'repository' before. It usually refers to some sort of collection. In the case of a cultural repository, it is a collection of all the information that is available concerning the cultural background of a person or a group of people.

Below, you will find an exercise with a few hints about how you can create your own personal cultural repository.

Before you start working on the exercise, let us quickly take a look at what makes a cultural repository. Basically, it comprises two parts:

- The first part includes **information about cultural dimensions**. If you have a specific purpose for your repository, you would choose a cultural system that looks at culture from a perspective that fits your goal. For example, if you are preparing yourself for a business meeting with a person from another country, you would choose a cultural system that looks at culture in a work context (e.g. the cultural system of Trompenaars and Hampden-Turner). If you are not pursuing a very specific goal, then you could choose a more general cultural model (e.g. the Hofstede cultural system).

- The second part of the cultural repository includes **information about the biographical background of the person or group for whom you are creating the repository**. Biographical information about a person could include their age, the countries where they grew up, their education, their foreign language skills, their experiences abroad, etc. It's a bit like a résumé, but with a special emphasis on aspects that influence culture (see also pp. 12-16 in Chapter 1). For a group of people (or a country as a whole), this could include historical information (for example, how the group was formed), the form of organization or government, or significant events.

It is not easy to create a cultural repository for another country, and it is probably even more difficult to gather relevant information for the cultural repository for another person. But don't get discouraged! Start with the information you know. Then think about what information you are missing and from where and how you could get it. Read, ask friends, and conduct research online. The more you can find out before your trip to another country or a personal encounter, the easier it will be for you to get started.

If you cannot find personal information about someone, you can start with general information about the person's country of origin. As soon as you get to know the person, you will have to adjust the information in their cultural repository anyway, because as we have discussed in this chapter, nobody corresponds completely to the culture of their country. So now it's your turn. Put together your own cultural repository.

YOUR OWN CULTURAL REPOSITORY

Remember the exercises in the earlier parts of this chapter, in which you compiled your cultural values for different cultural systems? If you have completed these exercises, you already have a large part of your cultural repository to hand (congratulations!). If you have not yet found time to complete these exercises, then try to find the cultural system that appeals to you most, and complete the corresponding exercise to fill in the first part of your cultural repository.

For the second (biographical) part of your cultural repository, fill in the information below (you can also print out a worksheet from the companion website of this book at *www.econcise.com/ CulturalSensitivityTraining*). This will give you the essential information that you will need for compiling your cultural repository.

You can also review your résumé, decide which parts are culturally relevant, and then transfer them to your cultural repository.

Biographical part of your cultural repository

General information

- *Age*
- *Nationality*
- *Education (What and where have you studied from kindergarten to university-level studies?)*
- *Studying/working abroad (Where? For how long?)*

Cultural background beyond cultural systems

- *In which countries have you lived, and for how long?*
- *What is the nationality of your parents, grandparents, etc. (if different from your own)?*
- *Which is/are your mother tongue(s)?*
- *What is/are your 'secondary' language(s)?*

KEY TAKEAWAYS FROM CHAPTER 2

1. Regardless of their culture, people ask the same **questions about life. But depending on their culture, they answer these questions differently.** Researchers have used this as a starting point to develop cultural systems.

2. **Each cultural system reflects the research interests of the researchers who developed them.** This also influences the potential field of application of these systems.

3. **Cultural systems can provide basic guidance, but never accurately describe an individual.** You will rarely find an individual person with a culture that is identical to their country's culture.

4. **No one is bound to the values that we can find in cultural systems.** We can react flexibly (within certain limits) and develop culturally, even as adults.

5. The **cultural repository** is a good way to better understand your own culture, but also to prepare for encounters with people from other countries or for a stay abroad.

6. **Inform yourself about the country and its people before a trip or meeting,** and be prepared that not all information that you find will prove true. Then correct your knowledge based on the new information that you acquire on site.

Notes for Chapter 2

1   Hofstede (2001); Hofstede et al. (2010).
2   e.g. Gruber (2011).
3   Schwartz (2012).
4   Inglehart (2018).
5   Schwartz (2012).
6   Davidov (2008).
7   Chhokar et al. (2019); House et al. (2013).
8   Kluckhohn and Strodtbeck (1961).
9   Ibid.
10 Trompenaars and Hampden-Turner (1998).
11 Ibid.
12 Hall (1973; 1977; 1982); Hall and Hall (1990).
13 Lewis (2018).

3

Realize: Motivation, personal traits, comparison with others, and the inner team

This chapter enables you to:

» Make assumptions about the culture of other groups or people and be aware of the tentativeness of these assumptions.
» Recognize differences between your culture, motives, needs, and personality traits and those of other people or groups of people in a non-judgmental way, and assess the opportunities and risks of similarities and differences between these elements.
» Develop a sense of how you normally react to people from another culture.

After familiarizing ourselves with our cultural characteristics (both on an individual and group level) in Chapter 2, this chapter is about **personal characteristics** which also influence our behavior in intercultural situations.

We will **compare our cultural and personal characteristics with those of other people**. This will enable us to **predict opportunities and risks for joint work** that arise from similarities and differences in these characteristics.

In the first part of this chapter, we will take a look at needs, motives, and the meaning of work. The second part of this chapter is about personality traits. Finally, in the third part, we will turn to our inner world of thoughts.

I would recommend you work on this chapter together with some of your friends, colleagues, or fellow students. If this is not possible, you will find some hints in the exercises for how you can still make some comparative evaluations.

Let's get started with a first exercise.

EXERCISE

COMPARE YOUR OWN CULTURAL RESPOSITORY WITH THAT OF OTHERS

Take at least one of the cultural profiles that you developed for yourself in the exercises in the previous chapter. Compare it to the corresponding profiles of your friends, colleagues, or fellow students. In which cultural dimensions are the profiles very similar? Where do you find differences? What could this imply if you had to work together in a team? Remember that similarities, as well as differences, can lead to both opportunities and risks.

If you are working through this book on your own, you can compare your own profile with the sample profiles on the companion website of this book at *www.econcise.com/CulturalSensitivityTraining*.

Motivation and needs

The term '**motivation**' describes the reason that drives people to start or continue an activity (or also the reason for not doing something). We are all motivated by motives (or 'driving forces'). One motive (or 'need') could, for example, be to have a slim body. This motive can motivate us to eat less and exercise more. In this sense, motives urge us to act.

The 'need' to have a slim body is an example of a **conscious motive** that we are consciously aware of. There are also **unconscious motives**, inner impulses and drives which we are not fully aware of (e.g. when a child tries to fulfill the unrealized dreams of their parents through choosing a profession that is not really in line with their own potential).

Motivation influences our perception, attention, and emotions. When we are setting ourselves a goal, for example, we will consciously perceive objects that fit that goal more often. Such objects will attract our attention more than others. To continue our example from above, if our motive is to have a slim body and we have set ourselves the objective to exercise more, we would more often consciously notice advertisements for sports-wear or sports events, news about the opening of a new fitness center, or other similar information that would otherwise be of less interest to us.

You may wonder why motives and motivation are relevant to cultural sensitivity. It's because **motives and motivation can be socially transmitted or learned**. They therefore tend to be quite similar within the same social group.

Diverging motives can also make cooperation more difficult. If you are able to set a goal in such a way that it serves all of these diverging motives, you can release tremendous forces through joint work.

Motivation is divided into intrinsic and extrinsic motivation. With **intrinsic motivation**, the motives lie in the action itself. The action is perceived as fun, interesting, or challenging. With **extrinsic motivation**, the results of the action (such as money, power, affiliation, or avoiding punishment) are the motives.

Regulation by Deci and Ryan

Edward L. Deci and Richard M. Ryan, two researchers at the University of Rochester, took a closer look at the phenomenon of motivation.[1] They classified motivation according to the extent to which actions meet **people's needs for competence, social inclusion, and autonomy**. In this regard, they speak of 'regulation' (because they see motivation as the regulating force behind our actions), and assume that there are five forms of motivation: one intrinsic and four extrinsic ones.

YOUR MOTIVATION FOR READING THIS BOOK

While reading the following explanations, try to think about your own motivation for working through this book. Which of the following regulations would you see as the one that best describes your own motivation?

Let us look at these five forms of motivation (or 'regulation') in more detail:

- **External regulation.** If you are working through this book because it is an assignment in one of your courses in college or at university, and you would otherwise not be able to pass it, then you are acting with external regulation. It is the most extrinsic form of regulation. You act because of external pressure, either to get a reward or to avoid punishment.
- **Introjected regulation.** If you are working through this book because your teachers have said that it's good to understand intercultural sensitivity and you believe them, then you act with introjected regulation. You have understood the goal, you might also accept that your teachers probably know what they're talking about, but you are not really committed to the goal.
- **Identified regulation.** If you are working through this book because you have recognized for yourself that intercultural sensitivity is important for your career—but you would actually prefer to do something completely different—then you act with identified regulation. You are convinced that you should achieve the goal, but it is in contradiction to or in conflict with other goals that you have.
- **Integrated regulation.** If you work through this book because you feel that intercultural sensitivity is important for your career, it's just the right time to learn it, and nothing else is holding you back, then you act with integrated regulation. All signs point to 'Go,' but you are still acting because you are driven by the result, such as an advantage that you see for your future career.

- **Intrinsic regulation.** If you are working through this book because you are burning to know why people act so differently, and you would really like to understand how to use these differences positively for collaboration and creative problem solving, then you act with intrinsic regulation. That means that you are driven by the action itself. In this case, the action of learning is rewarding enough for you. You do not need any additional external rewards to get started.

You will probably approach this book with different levels of commitment depending on the type of regulation that drives you. Likewise, the type of motivation that team members experience can influence how they commit themselves to a group task (see the following exercise).

EXERCISE

DIFFERENT MOTIVES IN TEAMWORK

Imagine that you have to work as part of a team of three students. You are super enthusiastic about the task and could work on it day and night. You find the problem highly exciting and you really want to find a solution.

One student in your team comes from a country with a strong collectivist streak. He wants to do everything to make sure that everyone in your team feels comfortable, and that you solve your task well. He is convinced that your team's mission is fundamentally sound. However, a harmonious working atmosphere is also very important for him.

The third student is interested in getting a very good grade for this group work. Actually, she is not interested in anything else.

Briefly describe the different motives of the three team members according to the Deci and Ryan model. What difficulties could arise for you and your teammates from your differing motives? How could you make sure all three of you work well for the assignment and meet your respective needs?

Needs according to McClelland

While Deci and Ryan use the needs for competence, social inclusion, and autonomy to explain motivation for a specific task, David C. McClelland looks at the needs for power, achievement, and affiliation without reference to a specific task.[2]

If you can assess both what motivates your team members to work on the current team task (Deci and Ryan) and what drives them in everyday life (McClelland), this can give you valuable clues for designing effective collaboration.

Let us therefore take a look at McClelland's needs (you will probably also notice some similarities with Deci and Ryan's types of motivation).

McClelland has identified **three basic needs** that drive us in our lives: **the need for power, the need for achievement, and the need for affiliation**. These needs express a person's desires, hopes, and motives. They represent a positive expression of needs: a 'need toward something.' They are opposed by negative expressions of needs, which come in the form of fears and anxieties: a 'need away from something.' All people have these needs to some extent. We find these needs in all cultures, although sometimes with a slightly different interpretation of their meaning.

Need for power

People who have a strong need for power want to control the means of influencing others. They want to maintain that power and try to avoid inferiority. This need is also about creating strong feelings in other people and about maintaining prestige, dominance, opinion, influence, and competition. This is the positive, 'outward' component of the need for power.

The negative or 'avoidant' component of the need for power is fear: fear of losing your sources of power (but also of increasing your power and becoming too powerful), fear of exercising your own power (but also of someone else exercising power over you, and of becoming dependent), and fear of not being able to make a difference with your own power, or of feeling powerless. There's also the fear of being insignificant or rejected. If you are working with people with a need for power, try to include them in decisions and try to avoid giving them the feeling that they are powerless or becoming powerless.

Need for achievement

People who have a strong need for achievement want to reach goals, show their abilities, and build competence. They are usually very curious. Their own development and diverse behaviors and thought processes motivate them. It fascinates them when they can solve problems, achieve a high standard, and show their talent.

Their biggest fear is losing or making mistakes. If you are working with people with the need for achievement, try to acknowledge their achievements explicitly, and try not to contribute to a feeling of losing or doing something wrong.

Need for affiliation

People who have a strong need for affiliation want to become familiar and friendly with other people. Safety, care, and friendship are important to them. This need emerges when people meet and come into contact with each other. Of course, how a relationship develops always depends on the situation. But the need for affiliation can also have a decisive influence. The positive component of the need for affiliation manifests itself in a hope for connection, a willingness to shape interpersonal situations actively, and in situational optimism.

In contrast, the negative component is expressed in a fear of rejection and being left alone, a fear of doing something wrong, resignation, and disinterest. When you are working with people with a need for affiliation, try to pay attention to their contributions, integrate them into the group, and avoid triggering their fear of being worthless.

COMPARE YOUR OWN BASIC MOTIVATION
WITH THAT OF OTHERS

- **Step 1:** Draw three horizontal lines and label them with the names of McClelland's three needs. Label the left side of each line as a 'weak need' and the right side as a 'strong need.'
- **Step 2:** Carefully and calmly read the descriptions of the three needs, and consider to what extent they apply to you. Put a point on each line at the place where you see yourself located for each need.
- **Step 3:** Finally, connect the points with lines and get your needs profile. If you return to this exercise and feel that your choices could be refined, simply change them.

If you would like to determine how far each of the three needs apply to you using a questionnaire, you will find a link to an academic paper that contains a questionnaire at *www.econcise.com/CulturalSensitivityTraining*.

Now compare your needs profile with the corresponding profiles of your friends, colleagues, or fellow students. Where do you notice similarities and differences? What could this imply if you had to work together in a team? Remember that similarities, as well as differences, can lead to both opportunities and risks.

If you are working through this book on your own, you can compare your own profile with the sample profiles on the companion website of this book at *www.econcise.com/CulturalSensitivityTraining*.

Maslow's pyramid of needs

Abraham H. Maslow was an American psychologist who took a holistic view of people.[3] To his mind, human development was an essential part of a good life. Based on his observations and research in the US, Maslow defined five needs, which he arranged like a pyramid. His work is often interpreted in such a way that the needs on a lower level must be fulfilled first (at least to a certain degree) before the needs on the next level take precedence.

He arranged his '**pyramid of needs**' as follows:

- At the bottom are **physiological needs**, followed by **safety needs, love needs, and esteem needs**. Maslow describes these as deficiency needs, meaning that people strive for something that's lacking.
- At the top of the pyramid is the **need for self-actualization**. For Maslow, this need is a growth need (or a need that is 'unfulfillable'), meaning that people strive for it and gain satisfaction from getting closer to it, but never achieve it completely.

Maslow himself never claimed that his pyramid was scientifically sound. He wanted to start a discussion about needs and their prioritization. Indeed, scientific evidence to support Maslow's pyramid of needs is still lacking today. Other presentations of needs and their interrelationships have also been developed in the meantime. For example, Veronika Hucke states that the prioritization of needs changes in a 'wavelike' fashion and grows in connection with personal development.[4] Lower-level needs of the Maslow pyramid (e.g. safety or love needs) reach the point of their highest intensity earlier than higher-level needs (e.g. esteem needs).

When considering the **cross-cultural applicability of needs theories**, the main issue is not the needs, but the arrangement of those needs, for example in a hierarchy.

Maslow's pyramid reflects the Western culture in which Maslow conducted his study. In other cultures, needs may be arranged quite differently. For example, in China, individual needs are more strongly intertwined with the needs of society.

Edwin Nevis, who studied the needs of people in China, organizes the physiological needs and the need for belonging in the left and right-hand bottom corners of an equilateral triangle.[5] In the top corner, he places the need for self-actualization, but unlike in Maslow's theory not as an individualistic aspiration, but in the service of society. The middle of Nevis' triangle of 'Chinese needs' contains the need for safety. Presumably, the need to save face can be associated with this need for safety.

Because it is so important to remember that needs and motivation can differ considerably between people of different countries, I always ask students in my courses to draw their own needs structure. Very few resemble Maslow's pyramid of needs (see Figure 8 for an example).

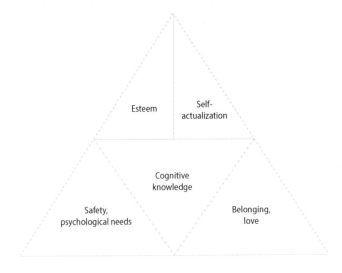

Figure 8 Example of an individual pyramid of needs

EXERCISE

COMPARE YOUR OWN BASIC MOTIVATION WITH THAT OF OTHERS

You have now learned a few ways in which needs can be related to each other. Think about your own needs and try to draw them in some kind of structure (e.g. a pyramid, a triangle, or any other kind of structure that you find appropriate for showing how your needs are interrelated).

Compare your own needs structure with those of your friends, colleagues, or fellow students. Where can you find similarities and differences? What could this imply if you had to work together in a team?

Remember that similarities, as well as differences, can lead to both opportunities and risks.

Consider saving the picture of your needs structure and coming back to it occasionally, to reflect on whether the structure might have changed at all given your recent experiences.

Motivation in the workplace

Up to this point, we have spoken about motivation mainly in the context of everyday life. Let us now take a closer look at the importance of **motivation in the workplace.**

What is the importance of work for people? First and foremost, work is a way to earn money to secure a livelihood. But with our work, we can also show our competence. It helps us to structure our days and gives us orientation in life. By working together with our colleagues, we are in contact with other people and experience social recognition, status, and prestige. Last but not least, work contributes to the formation of our personal identity.

All of this is also related to motives, motivation, and the fulfillment of needs. Thus, it is not surprising that **the meaning that people see in their work is also influenced by their cultural background.**

We can also see differences between cultures when interpreting what work is all about on a more general level. In some countries, for example, work is seen more like play and something 'easy,' whereas in other countries, work is more like a duty and equated with effort.

The meaning that employees ascribe to their work influences which needs they want to fulfill with their work. These needs also affect the significance of work for people. The significance or importance of work, in turn, determines whether employees are intrinsically or extrinsically motivated. And that again influences which needs employees strive to satisfy.

From our discussion of needs above, we know that needs influence motivation, which in turn determines how we behave as individuals as well as in groups. This process takes place against the background of our values and attitudes, as well as the norms of the society we have been socialized in. But it is also influenced by the culture of the organization or company we're working in.

This implies two things:

- On the one hand, employees bring their own meaning of work and their own motivation to work with them. They want to be accepted as they are. The company should therefore design working conditions in a way that meets the needs of employees. Employees want to be valued in their workplaces, and they should also be able to fulfill their needs there.
- On the other hand, the organizational culture influences employees' perception of the importance of work, and can meaningfully direct the motivation of employees and guide their actions. Thus, ideally, the aims of the employees and the targets of the company converge.

EXERCISE

THE MEANING OF WORK

Please think about what work means to you. In the explanations above, you will certainly find a few clues. But you can also go beyond that. To what extent do your work-related attitudes differ from your parents, friends, people from your country, and people from other countries with whom you have worked so far?

Compare your key points with your friends, colleagues, or fellow students. Where do you have the same views? Where do you see differences? And what might this imply if you were to work together in a team? Remember that similarities, as well as differences, can lead to both opportunities and risks.

If you are working through this book on your own, you can interview your relatives and friends to get some ideas about how different people define the meaning of their work in different ways.

Motivation and the cultural dimensions according to Hofstede

So far, we have not really considered the influence of culture on motivation. Let us therefore take a closer look at **motivation in the context of Hofstede's cultural system**. (The following ideas for how culture affects motivation are mainly derived from the descriptions of the cultural dimensions in Chapter 2. You can build up such a scheme for other cultural systems as well.)

How could people with a high or low level of the different cultural dimensions be motivated (at least in principle)? Helen Deresky tried to answer this question as follows:[6]

- People with a **high level of uncertainty avoidance** look for a safe workplace and for security at work. In such a culture, you would want to make sure that the workplace has a feeling of safety. You will involve people in decisions and let them shape their workplace as much as possible for themselves. If you would like to find out more about the potential pitfalls and risks of your project, ask people with high uncertainty avoidance—they usually have a good eye for threats.
- People with a **low level of uncertainty avoidance** love risk. They feel comfortable working on innovative projects, where they are able to try out and implement new things.
- People with a **high level of power distance** prefer to work in hierarchies. They like to have clear instructions and boundaries at work. The prospect of being able to gain a promotion can motivate them if they have a corresponding need for power. If you are the leader of such a person, you might want to give explicit instructions and manage their execution of the task.
- In contrast, people with a **low level of power distance** need a team and peers around them to feel comfortable at work. They enjoy working with others and being inspired by them. They don't do well with instructions, no matter whether they're giving or receiving them. They thrive when working on mutual tasks.
- Very **individualistically oriented people** prefer to work autonomously and in a self-determined manner. This does not prevent them from teaming up with colleagues for certain work. But they

like to make decisions by themselves, depending on what they think is right for the current task. As their leader, you would want to give them as much freedom as possible to complete their tasks.

- Very **collectivistically oriented people** feel more comfortable in groups. They not only want to collaborate with colleagues on a task, but have real interpersonal contact with them. They look for loyalty in the team. Try to create an appropriate group atmosphere for these people.
- People with a **high masculinity index** care about the traditional division of roles. It will be difficult to get their support when you push them toward a behavior that they see as lying outside of the usual role definition. They will usually feel much more comfortable if they can perform tasks that correspond to their gender role. This is perfectly fine as long as no-one is discriminated against.
- People with a **low masculinity index** (i.e. a high degree of 'femininity') feel more comfortable when all employees account for tasks equally and take part in everything. Make sure that there are equal opportunities for all employees, and that everyone can combine their work and family commitments. The corporate culture can influence the values, attitudes, and norms of employees in the interest of equality.

Please remember that these descriptions are no more than **rough guidelines** or 'average' tendencies of a person. They must always be adapted to the individual person and the concrete situation. In addition, these descriptions refer to one cultural dimension at a time, when in reality, all the dimensions are interacting with—and sometimes also contradicting—each other. Be careful, therefore, to take these descriptions as an initial reference point that you will need to check, correct and embellish through trial and error.

In the following exercise, you can assess to what extent Deresky's descriptions apply to you.

MOTIVATION AT WORK

Return to your cultural profile according to Hofstede that you completed in Chapter 2.

Read through Deresky's descriptions of what motivates people according to Hofstede's dimensions again and determine how you 'should' be motivated based on your classification in each dimension. Make some notes about this.

Then consider to what extent you think this way of motivating yourself could be successful. Does everything fit? What does not fit? How could you use such general guidelines in your own efforts to motivate other people?

Personality traits

People differ in their **personal characteristics**. They are loud or quiet, cautious or daredevil, orderly or messy, and many other things besides. Some of these characteristics are very stable and do not change (or change only slowly) over a lifetime. But they affect how we live our lives, and how we think, act, and feel. Therefore, we should also take a look at personal characteristics when we want to get a sense of why different people act in certain ways.

What are these personal characteristics and where do they come from? And how can we tell how pronounced a trait is in a person?

There's an old debate around whether a person's characteristics are inherited (i.e. biologically determined) or acquired (i.e. socially determined). It is generally assumed that biological predispositions, basic inclinations, personal experiences, and external influences (especially social influences) together shape the development of a person's personality.

So far, we have discussed the social influences. Let us now take a closer look at the more 'biological' influences. It's worth mentioning, however, that these are at least partly socially shaped, too.

Even in ancient times, people were interested in pinpointing and categorizing what the basic human characteristics are. Thus, a wide variety of personality models have been developed over many years, some of them credible, others less so. Some models border on charlatanism. Therefore, if somebody asks you to take a personality test, always ask them first to explain in which (scientific) basis it is grounded and what purpose it is supposed to serve.

The 'Big Five' personality model

For this book we will use the **'Big Five' personality model**.[7] It is considered the most reliable model for personality and is used in many scientific studies.

A lexical approach was used to derive the model.[8] That means that the researchers first looked at words that are used to describe human characteristics, and how often they were used in connection with other specific words.[9] Using statistical methods such as principal component analysis, five components were found. One personality trait was then assigned to each of these five components.

As with all widely used models, it has not remained uncriticized. Some critics, for example, doubt that this model can describe personality in a sufficiently differentiated way. However, if we want to recognize the **basic personality tendencies of a person**, the 'Big Five' model can be a very useful tool.

In this model, there are five characteristics that describe a person (hence the name of the model). These traits are **O**penness to experience, **C**onscientiousness, **E**xtraversion, **A**greeableness, and **N**euroticism. In English this forms the acronym OCEAN, which is why the name **'OCEAN model'** is often used, too.

Let's look at these five traits in more detail:[10]

- **Openness** to experience describes the extent to which people are interested in new experiences and learning new things. It also describes the extent to which they consciously seek situations that provide them with such experiences. Open-minded people are inventive and curious, and they love variety. People with a lower degree of openness are typically more cautious and conservative, and they prefer to build on the tried and tested.

- **Conscientiousness** describes the extent to which people are precise and purposeful, and how they are able to control themselves. People with higher levels of conscientiousness organize their work carefully. They plan a lot and appear reliable and deliberate. People with lower levels of conscientiousness act spontaneously and lightheartedly. Therefore, they sometimes appear careless and inaccurate.
- **Extraversion** describes how people approach each other. Extroverts are sociable, talkative, optimistic, and stimulated by others. Introverts appear more reserved, withdrawn, and independent. They tend to act alone rather than together with others.
- **Agreeableness** describes how people behave in interactions. Agreeable people are interested in the well-being of others. They tend to be compassionate, friendly, helpful, cooperative, and compliant. People with lower levels of agreeableness tend to look out for their own interests. They are more argumentative, love competition, and can also appear distrustful and self-centered.
- **Neuroticism** describes how people experience negative emotions. Neurotic people tend to be nervous, insecure, sad, and feel fear and worry. They do not withstand stress well. Some authors refer to this expression of the trait as 'emotional lability.' People with lower levels of neuroticism usually appear more calm, stable, relaxed, and self-confident. They are able to cope with stressful situations confidently. Some authors refer to this expression of the trait as 'emotional stability' or 'ego strength.'

There are several questionnaires available for measuring the 'Big Five' personality traits. Some of them measure emotional stability rather than neuroticism (where high values of emotional stability would mean low values of neuroticism). This often leads to confusion. Pay close attention, therefore, when you use such a questionnaire.

YOUR 'BIG FIVE' PERSONALITY TRAITS

In this exercise, you will analyze your own personality traits according to the 'Big Five' model.

Draw five horizontal lines and label them with the names of the five traits. Write 'low' on the left side and 'high' on the right side of each line.

Carefully and calmly read the descriptions of the characteristics above, and consider to what extent they apply to you. Place a dot on each line at the point where you see yourself in this trait. Finally, you can connect the points and get your personality profile according to the 'Big Five' model. If you return to this exercise and feel that your choices could be refined, simply change them.

There are countless free tests online that you can use to determine your personality traits. At the time of writing, a scientifically valid and reliable test is available at *http://ipip.ori.org* (follow the link "The IPIP-NEO"). The set of questions that are offered here are commonly used in scientific studies.

Once you have taken a personality test, consider the following questions: Did you assess yourself accurately when creating your personality profile using the descriptions of the traits above? If not, why not? What might this mean when you try to assess the traits of other people?

EXERCISE

COMPARE YOUR OWN PERSONALITY PROFILE
WITH THOSE OF OTHERS

Take your personality profile from the previous exercise and compare it with the profiles of your friends, colleagues, or fellow students. Where can you find similarities and differences? What could this imply if you had to work together in a team? Remember that similarities, as well as differences, can lead to both opportunities and risks.

If you are working through this book on your own, compare your own personality profile with the sample profiles you can find on the companion website of this book at *www.econcise.com/CulturalSensitivityTraining*.

Basic orientations of the human being according to Riemann and Thomann

Fritz Riemann, a German psychoanalyst, identified **four basic forms of anxiety**.[11] Christoph Thomann, a Swiss psychologist, labeled them with two polarizing pairs of terms.[12] The resulting representation of the two polarizing pairs of terms in a rectangular coordinate system is called the **Riemann–Thomann model**.

Thomann used this model to explain to his clients what might be behind their behaviors. Because it is well suited to describing human behavior in general, it can also **help us interpret people's behavior in cross-cultural situations**.

The Riemann–Thomann model is not a model for characterizing or describing personality types, as we have seen with the 'Big Five' model. It is therefore not possible to fully describe a personality with it. However, it contains **a person's basic orientations** which are of particular importance in interactions with other people. Some basic orientations also have special significance in conflicts. Therefore, the model is well suited to interpreting critical situations and is also used to resolve conflicts.

The four basic orientations of the model can be assigned to two dimensions: a temporal and a spatial dimension. The temporal dimension comprises the two poles of **duration and change**, and the spatial dimension comprises the two poles of **proximity and distance**.

A person's basic orientations influence how they feel, behave, communicate, and shape their relationships. Each pole has both positive and negative aspects, but no alignment is inherently wrong or negative.

If the **distance orientation** of people is high, they want to separate themselves from others. They look for independence, individuality, and freedom. They think and act rationally and often appear cool and aloof. To get involved with others, people with a high distance orientation need sufficient opportunities to withdraw and to feel that they are not tied to these people.

Proximity orientation is the opposite pole of distance orientation. People with a high proximity orientation need trust, security, harmony, bonding, and closeness. They are sociable and understanding. They can easily identify with others and forget about themselves. Since people with a high proximity orientation dislike being alone, they risk becoming dependent on others.

People with high **duration orientation** are punctual, reliable, responsible, and careful. They love plans, control, laws, and commitment. Stability and permanence are important to them. For some people, this can make them seem boring, inflexible, and stubborn.

Change orientation is the opposite pole of duration orientation. People with a high change orientation love novelty, changing stimuli, and spontaneity. They are imaginative, creative, and fanciful. This sometimes makes them seem chaotic or unreliable to other people.

We have all four basic orientations in each of us, emphasized in varying degrees, and this specific emphasis can be thought of as our basic profile. Around this profile, our orientations can move depending on the situation. The goal of personality development is to expand the area around our profile in order to enable us to respond more flexibly to different situations. (This is quite similar to what we discussed regarding our adaptability to culture on pp. 60-62 in Chapter 2).

YOUR POSITION IN THE RIEMANN–THOMANN MODEL

Draw a rectangular coordinate system. Label the vertical axis with the two poles for the spatial dimension: 'duration' at the top and 'change' at the bottom. Label the horizontal axis with the two poles for the time dimension: 'proximity' at the left end and 'distance' at the right end. Now consider where your general orientation lies and place a point in the corresponding position.

Compare your coordinate system with those of your friends, colleagues, or fellow students. You can also transfer their points onto your own coordinate system. Are your points close together or far apart? What could this imply if you had to work together in a team? Remember that both points that are close together and points that are far apart can mean opportunities as well as risks.

Consider saving your coordinate system and coming back to it occasionally, to reflect on whether your orientation might have changed given your recent experiences.

If you are working through this book on your own, compare your own coordinate system with the sample systems on the companion website of this book at *www.econcise.com/CulturalSensitivityTraining*.

Thinking and discussion styles

People think in different ways. Which of these **thinking styles** we use in discussions is not really a personality trait. It is essentially dependent on our previous experiences and our socialization. In discussions with others, we learn which ways of thinking are helpful to reach the best results. Later on, we mostly unconsciously apply these learned ways of thinking. How we think in discussions influences our communication behavior. Let us therefore take a look at different ways of thinking in discussions in a bit more detail.

Edward de Bono categorizes our ways of thinking in discussions into six perspectives, which he calls the '**six thinking hats**':[13]

1. Neutral **analytical thinking** focuses on facts, data, and figures. There is no subjective evaluation involved.
2. Subjective **emotional thinking** is characterized by personal opinions and feelings. Contradictions are possible when we think emotionally.
3. Someone who uses factual arguments to either draw attention to negative aspects and risks or raise objections is **thinking critically** (or even pessimistically).
4. In contrast, **realistic thinkers** point out positive aspects in their arguments. They also look for objective possibilities and advantages.
5. With **innovative thinking**, you put different ideas together and develop creative suggestions and new ideas from them.
6. A person who follows an **ordering thinking** approach wants to create order through structuring ideas and thoughts and creating a systematic overview.

If you want to hold an effective discussion, try to bring together people with different thinking styles. Each person's way of thinking will contribute to the outcome in a specific way. If you miss a 'hat' in your discussion group, ask somebody to deliberately put on the missing 'hat' by consciously trying to adopt that missing thinking style.

THINKING HATS

Try to answer the following questions:

- Which one or two of de Bono's thinking hats do you usually wear during a discussion?
- What hats do your friends, colleagues, or fellow students wear?
- What happens when you have a discussion with someone who wears the same hats as you do?
- What happens when you have a discussion with someone who wears completely different hats to you?
- What is a good mix of hats for a group discussion?

The 'inner team'

Have you ever talked to yourself? It's not that rare or weird. As we have seen so far, there are so many things that drive us—so many external factors and internal thought processes that influence us—that it is quite normal if you cannot take a clear position on every single issue you encounter. There are always pros and cons to consider when we think about a difficult issue. In such a case, we enter into an **inner dialogue**, trying to 'negotiate' the different positions within ourselves to come to a conclusive decision.

Schulz von Thun illustrates these internal thought processes in his **model of the 'inner team.'**[14] The main intention of this model is to enable you to **observe and direct your own inner thought processes**, to lead them to a good result.

If you want to get an overview of where you stand in a situation, make a difficult decision, or question your feelings, the model of the 'inner team' can help you to sort your thoughts, see things more clearly, and in the end being more true to yourself.

How does the inner team work in practice?

Imagine you have to write an essay which is due to be submitted in two days. Your friend calls and invites you to the cinema. How do you react? You probably immediately hear several 'voices' within yourself. One of them says that you have to write a solid essay because you need a good grade. Another voice wants to be a kind buddy and not disappoint your friend. And maybe there is a third voice that says you have done enough for today and deserve a little relaxation. All these voices are there, and they all want to be accepted. In the long run, it is damaging to try to suppress any of these voices. With the 'inner team' model, you can now make all of these voices heard. You can give them room.

EXERCISE

LEARN HOW TO DRAW AN INNER TEAM

Take a piece of paper and a pen. As you read through the following paragraphs, complete each step on the paper in front of you.

Draw a torso with a head. This is you. If you want to, give yourself hair, ears, and a face. You can also write your name besides the figure. Then draw a big thought bubble that represents the thought process that is going on inside you.

Taking the example from above (the friend who invites you to the cinema), go through your inner voices again. Let's start with the one that wants to continue working. For this voice, draw a little figure (a torso with a head) inside the large thought bubble. Give this figure a name (maybe it is 'the responsible one'). In a speech bubble, write the main thought of this figure, i.e. that it wants to deliver a high-quality essay in two days' time.

Now consider the second voice: the one that wants to be a good friend. Draw a corresponding figure in the thought bubble and give it a name (e.g. 'the actual friend'). In a speech bubble, write the main thought of this figure, i.e. that it doesn't want to disappoint a friend.

The third voice is the one which would like to relax. This one also gets a figure in the thought bubble and a name. Maybe this is the one that takes care of yourself, so perhaps you could call it 'the caretaker.' In a speech bubble, write the main thought of this figure, i.e. that you deserve a little relaxation.

This is your 'inner team'! The team members now need to decide whether you should go to the cinema with your friend or continue writing your essay (see Figure 9).

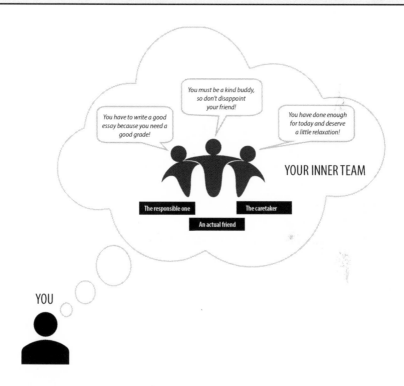

Figure 9 An example of an inner team

Sometimes it is enough to just visualize your different views on a situation to gain more clarity about a decision. If not, you can now let your inner team enter into a dialogue. Schulz von Thun recommends introducing a team leader for this purpose (and then assigning that team leader a figure in your thought bubble in the exercise above). The team leader moderates the discussion and makes the final decision.

Listen to how each voice justifies its position. Also, consider what each voice would say it needed if it 'lost.' You might also want to suggest compromises. Maybe the 'caretaker' can agree on continuing to work for a defined time and then doing something together with your friend. If it would be too late to go to the cinema by then, you could propose some other activity. Discuss with your voices until you come to a decision that considers all positions.

After a good discussion, the decision should cause you fewer concerns. You should then also be able to present the decision to your friend authentically and clearly.

EXERCISE

USE THE INNER TEAM FOR YOUR OWN SITUATION

Now try using your inner team for your own situation. You can use any situation in which you are (or have been) unclear about how to make a decision. If nothing comes to your mind, you could consider how you would feel about a semester abroad or a longer work period abroad. What would push you abroad? What would keep you at home? Would you have any concerns or wishes?

Discuss your situation with your friends, colleagues, or fellow students and explain the inner team you have drawn. The more often you try this, the easier it will be for you to make your inner voices heard. After some time, you will no longer need to draw a sketch to illustrate your inner team; you'll simply be able to consider their positions while thinking about the situation.

You will find a template you can use to draw your inner team on the companion website of this book at
www.econcise.com/CulturalSensitivityTraining.

Using the inner team in a cross-cultural context

If you are undecided about how to assess or react in a certain situation, remember to consider your inner team. We can also view intercultural situations as decision-making situations, as you will have to decide how to interact with people from other cultures. In such situations, you will also encounter 'inner voices' like the ones we have discussed in the situations above.

In **intercultural situations**, there are **four additional 'voices'** in your inner team:[15]

- We have a voice within us that represents our **own cultural background**: a part of us that would like to be perceived as representing our culture in the sense of simply 'being this way.'
- Then there is the voice that **finds other cultures interesting and exciting** and wants to find out new things about them.
- But there is also the voice that is full of **stereotypical knowledge about the other culture** (consider what we discussed about the origins and functions of stereotypes at the beginning of Chapter 1).
- Last, but not least—perhaps a bit quieter than the other voices, but still present—there is a voice that represents **the other culture within us**. That's the voice that feels somewhat representative of the other culture, where we have an overlap with the other culture, and where it's clear to us how the other culture interacts.

To summarize, against the background of your own voices, you will perceive how people from other cultures act, communicate, and treat you as follows:

- you always react as the representative of your own culture,
- and as someone who is curious about the other culture,
- spontaneously based on your stereotypical knowledge,
- and based on the knowledge that you have of the other culture.

EXERCISE

REACTIONS OF THE INNER VOICES IN RELATION TO A DIFFERENT CULTURE

If you come from a culture where it is customary to arrive at the agreed time, imagine that you have arranged to meet for dinner with a person from a country with a more relaxed perception of time. That person arrives half an hour late and doesn't say a word of apology because they think their behavior is quite normal.

If you come from a culture where time is more of a 'guideline', imagine that you are meeting for dinner with a person with a strict perception of time. You are half an hour late and that person calls you unreliable and is angry with you.

How do your four inner 'intercultural' voices react? How can they come to an agreement to make you react authentically in the situation?

In the next chapter, we will take a look at how to resolve intercultural conflict situations. In such situations, remember to think about your inner voices and let them have their say (as in the exercises above). In this way, you can determine whether you have been able to resolve a critical situation authentically and satisfactorily for yourself.

KEY TAKEAWAYS FROM CHAPTER 3

1. **Knowing our own cultural background** helps us better understand other people and groups and to see both similarities and differences between us.

2. **Motives and needs** influence whether and how we act. If people collaborate and their actions are based on different needs, this can lead to problems.

3. Try to **organize the joint work of people with different needs** in such a way that the needs of all team members are fulfilled to a large extent.

4. Although work has the same basic functions everywhere, **people sometimes interpret the meaning of work differently.**

5. Our basic **personality traits** are partly inherited, but also socially (and thus culturally) determined.

6. The 'inner team' can help us gain clarity about our own needs and represent our own point of view in communication situations authentically.

Notes for Chapter 3

1　Ryan and Deci (2017).
2　McClelland (1961).
3　Maslow (1943).
4　Hucke (2019).
5　Nevis (1983).
6　Based on Deresky (2016).
7　Neyer and Asendorpf (2018).
8　See for example Goldberg (1990).
9　See for example a list of 18,000 property words by Allport and Odbert (1936).
10　Neyer and Asendorpf (2018).
11　Riemann (2013).
12　Thomann and Schulz von Thun (2003).
13　de Bono (1992).
14　Schulz von Thun (2013).
15　Kumbier (2006).

Relate: Resolving difficult situations and effective intercultural communication

....

This chapter enables you to:

» Familiarize yourself with different models and tools for interpreting and resolving intercultural conflict situations, as well as their possible areas of application.
» Apply communication and conflict management models and tools to your own situations.
» Evaluate which elements of a communication situation could lead to misinterpretations and find out how to prevent this.

....

At the beginning of this chapter, let us recap what we have discussed so far. In Chapter 1, **we learned that we always act and react automatically and unconsciously** to a certain extent. From Chapter 2, we know that **we have been shaped by the environment in which we grew up** and are therefore influenced by our different cultures. In Chapter 3, we saw that as human beings, in addition to being influenced by the culture we've been socialized in, **we also have different traits and needs**. We compared how our own 'being this way' relates to and differs from those of others, and in the exercises we tried to derive opportunities and risks from our similarities and differences. Getting to know our 'inner team' helped us to **take a first step toward resolving critical situations** by trying to first create clarity within ourselves.

Let us now step out and face other people. As soon as we meet others, our different traits, desires, needs, and cultural backgrounds meet, too. We might start wondering about certain unfamiliar aspects of these situations. The unfamiliarity can make us feel uncomfortable, and we would maybe like to change such situations. I will call these situations '**critical situations**' (sometimes, they are also referred to as 'critical incidents').

Critical situations are always connected with **communication** or, in more general terms, with **interaction**. In this chapter, we will therefore first take a look at what communication is and what factors we need to consider in a communication situation. Then we will explore how we can interpret communication problems, and how to identify their causes and meaning. Thereafter, we will consider a few specific aspects of communication, and you will also learn some ways to resolve difficult communication problems. At the end of this chapter, I will summarize a few strategies for successful intercultural communication.

The communication process

The basic communication process is quite simple. There is nothing really sophisticated about it. **A sender wants to convey a message to a receiver and uses a transmission medium to do so.**[1]

Let's take this book here as an example. I am the sender. You are the receiver. In the previous chapter, I wanted to get a message across to you—I wanted to explain what the 'inner team' is all about. In order to achieve my aim, I first had to present the content of my message (i.e. what the inner team is) in a meaningful way. This is called **encoding**.

I chose a text written in English to achieve my purpose. I could just as well have recorded a podcast or a video, or I could have written the text in my native language of German instead. In order to get my message across to you, we need a **transmission medium**. Together with my publisher, we decided that a book would be the appropriate format for my content (with paper as a transmission medium if you are reading a paperback version, or an electronic transmission medium in the case of the e-book version).

For the message to reach you, you have to read the text and make sense of it. This is called **decoding** (and more probably than not my native language would not have been the best choice here, unless you're fluent in German).

Whether you know and understand what the inner team is after reading my text depends on many things which are related either to the sender (me), the receiver (you), or the transmission medium. Everything that can interfere with the communication process in a negative way is called **noise**. If you are a student, it's not only up to you to fully understand something (although you indeed play an important role in the process). If the speaker is rambling in a way that you cannot understand, there's noise in the encoding. If other participants in the room are too noisy, there's (real) noise that disturbs the transmission medium (spoken language transmitted through the air).

Let's inspect this concept of noise in a bit more detail. Consider our example from above again. When I wrote about the inner team, I did so in light of what I know, and I made assumptions about what you already know. I explained it in the way I think you can best understand it. And of course, my writing was also shaped by how other texts that I have read are written.

It's similar for you when you read the text. You have a certain amount of previous knowledge about the subject. If I overestimate that amount, my explanation won't be detailed enough. If I underestimate it, my explanation will be too detailed. Either way, this can cause problems: if I give you too little or too much information, it could make it difficult for you to understand the text. I risk confusing you, boring you or overwhelming you.

I am also used to a certain style of writing, and so are you. If our styles do not match, it may be difficult for you to understand the content of the text.

This means that both the sender and receiver communicate based on their prior experiences, expectations, perceptions, values, and norms. It means that **sending and receiving messages is culturally influenced**. Therefore, the better we understand the cultural background and personal preferences of our communication partners, the better we can prevent misunderstandings (or are at least able to recognize and eliminate them more quickly).

The communication channel can also cause misunderstandings. On the one hand, there can be simple technical aspects, like smudged paper or a flickering screen. Thus, you simply do not see the text, which means that you obviously cannot perceive or interpret it. On the other hand, the choice of the communication channel and the way we deal with certain forms of transmission media can also be culturally influenced.

EXERCISE

YOUR OWN EXAMPLE OF A COMMUNICATION PROCESS

Come up with your own example of a communication process. Who is the sender, and who is the receiver? What content is transmitted via which medium? How does the sender encode the content? How does the receiver decode the content? What factors can affect your mutual understanding?

Discuss your example with your friends, colleagues, or fellow students. What other ideas do they have about factors that can interfere with the communication process?

Let us now take a brief look at the psychological processes that are taking place when we receive information:

- First, we have to **perceive** the content. Depending on the communication channel, we hear, see, or touch the message.
- Then we have to **interpret** what we perceive, i.e. we attach a meaning to the perception. By now, you already know that our cultural and personal background plays a crucial role in that process.
- As soon as we have attached a meaning to what we perceive, we **feel** something. This is also influenced by our individual preferences.

These three processes primarily take place **unconsciously**. But it is still possible to influence these processes, and we can practice consciously perceiving the cultural influences at play.

If you realize that an interaction did not work as planned, take some time to think about what went wrong, and what you can learn about how to prevent such situations in the future. If you practice this more often, you will soon be able to more consciously consider what to do in such a situation as soon as you recognize a similar problem.

Resolving difficult interactions

There are different ways of interpreting and resolving difficult interactions. Some methods are more general, while others consider specific aspects of such situations. Develop an overview of the different methods first, and then select the tool or option that is most appropriate for the situation you want to investigate.

Let us start with a general framework for analyzing difficult interactions ('general' meaning that it is equally suitable for all types of conflictual situations).

A general framework for analyzing difficult interactions

This framework includes the following four steps (see Figure 10 below):

- **Step 1—Observation:** Write down what actually happened: what you saw and heard. Stick to the facts. What was the situation like, objectively speaking? Where did it take place? Who was involved? Then describe how the people involved behaved. Again, stick to simply describing what you observed. You cannot know what the other people were thinking or feeling or why they behaved the way they did. Try to use neutral wording.
- **Step 2—Your own feelings:** Recall how you felt in the situation. Which actions of the people involved influenced you and in what way? What feelings did they trigger in you? How did you react to them? What moved you emotionally? What was different from what you expected? What seemed unusual to you? Try not to judge your feelings. They are there and have to be respected as they are.

- **Step 3—Interpretation:** Try to find plausible reasons for the behavior of the people involved. Take one person at a time (and don't forget yourself). Consider the cultural and personal backgrounds of these people. Remember the tools from Chapters 2 and 3. Pick out the models, dimensions, and characteristics that seem appropriate for your situation. With a little practice, you will soon develop a good sense of which aspects of the models are helpful in which situations. Once you have gathered all your thoughts about all the people involved, revisit your description of the situation from the first step. Go through each action taken and consider to what extent the cultural or personal backgrounds of the people involved might have influenced their actions. Where was a person's behavior quite 'normal' based on their culture, but very unusual for you, maybe not purposeful in that situation, or perhaps even harmful? Also think about what might have triggered your feelings. Don't forget your own cultural and personal background in your analysis.

- **Step 4—Solution:** Think about how you can resolve these difficult interactions or prevent them from occurring again in the future. If you were in such a situation again, how could you react differently to not let it become problematic? Imagine a few behaviors that you could apply so that you are prepared for the worst-case scenario. Sometimes a minor change in behavior on your part can help to transform a difficult situation into a more solvable one. Also think of possible precautionary measures that you could take to prevent an unpleasant development of a communication situation from the very beginning. Sometimes it helps if the reaction of another person is no longer unexpected for you. You may have already achieved this level of understanding by interpreting previous communication situations. But please do not forget that you cannot change other people. You can only decide to change your own behavior (even if your cultural and personal background will remain the same or change only slowly).

If you want to use this framework to analyze a particular interaction, you can use the template on the companion website of this book at *www. econcise.com/CulturalSensitivityTraining.*

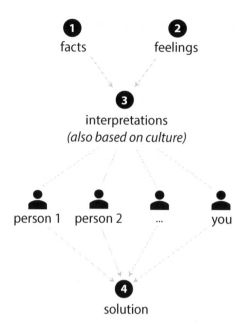

Figure 10 How to resolve difficult interactions

Here are some additional notes about applying this framework:

- Remember that **your interpretation is always based on your personal ideas about other people**. You can never be sure that people really are as you imagine them to be. Consider that your own cultural and personal background always influences all your own thoughts as well.
- With a thoughtful interpretation of the situation, you will at least be able to **discover basic starting points for explaining why the situation might not have turned out quite as you wanted it to**. The more familiar you are with the people you are communicating with, the more accurate your interpretations will usually be.
- You can also consider **making your assumptions explicit** in your conversations with others. Be careful and sensitive here, however, because it is not common in all cultures to talk about inner realities.

Now that you have familiarized yourself with the general framework for analyzing difficult interactions, let us take a look at three additional tools that you might find helpful for interpreting and finding solutions for conflict situations in an intercultural context.

The 'communication square' (or 'four-sides model')

As already mentioned, communication is not only about the content of the message. The German psychologist and communication expert Friedemann Schulz von Thun summarized the four most important aspects of communication in his 'communication square', also widely known as the 'four-sides model' of communication.[2]

In this model, each of the four sides of the square represents one aspect of communication. For visual clarity, four different colors stand for the four aspects:

- blue for the **factual aspect**,
- green for the **relationship aspect**,
- yellow for the **self-revelation aspect**,
- and red for the **appeal aspect**.

On the left side of the square there's the sender, and on the right side the receiver, so that a message 'flows' from left to right. (If you are used to a language which is written from the right to the left, your message could flow instead from right to left).

The **factual aspect** contains the core content—what the message is intended to inform someone about. The **relationship aspect** clarifies the relationship that the sender sees themselves as having with to the receivers of the message. The **self-revelation aspect** contains what the sender says about themselves by conveying the message. Finally, the **appeal aspect** expresses what the sender wants from the receiver.

Now let us consider the four aspects again to look more precisely at what each of them mean for both the sender and receiver:

- On the **factual level**, the sender wants to inform the receiver about something. This is what the receiver is supposed to understand.
- On the **relationship level**, the sender conveys how they see their relationship with the receiver: what they think about them, and how

they think they are getting along with them. From the way that the sender communicates, the receiver can also 'read' how the sender is evaluating them.

- The **self-revelation aspect** represents what the sender wants to reveal about themselves. The receiver will try to find out more about this 'hidden' part of the message and what it tells them about the sender.
- The **appeal level** contains what the sender wants the receiver to do. The receiver has to find out what is expected of them.

All aspects except the factual one are usually conveyed rather unconsciously and implicitly—and even the factual content is not transmitted with equal clarity, distinctiveness, and directness in all cultures.

All too often, we do not pay enough attention to the relationship aspect of communication. This often leads to bad feelings and miscommunication.

There are two scenarios in which the four-sides model is especially useful:

- You can use it **to analyze a conversation** that did not go well. In this case, you would go through the critical sentences that you remember with the help of the model and try to identify the potential causes of the misunderstandings.
- You can use it **to prepare for a critical conversation**. Take the sentences that you fear could be misunderstood or where it is important that they are understood correctly, and consider what you are going to say with the help of the four sides of the communication square. Of course, you will need to guess a bit here about how your counterpart might understand and respond to the things you say.

You can also use the **cultural models** that we discussed in Chapter 2—especially the cultural dimensions related to communication and interpersonal relationships—to support your interpretations.

A side-effect of using the four-sides model to prepare for a conversation is that you can mentally adjust to your communication partners (and, in principle, to their culture), thus being able to react more appropriately to unexpected questions. The more often you practice using the communication square, the easier it will be and the more precise your assessments will become.

Before I suggest an exercise on the four-sides model, I would like to give you an example of how you can analyze a situation that did not go so well. There's often friction between parents and their adolescent children. Let's presume a mother says to her teenage daughter, "You need a haircut. Your hair looks terrible." What could the mother as the sender have meant and what could the daughter as the receiver have understood?

The message on the factual level is the same for both: a new haircut is due. The mother doesn't like the current one. On the relationship level, the mother might have meant that as a mother, she wants to give her daughter well-intentioned advice. The daughter could have understood that she is seen as a small child that is being given an instruction. As self-revelation, the mother might have wanted to express that she cares about her daughter's well-being, and that she does not want her to be laughed at because of an inappropriate haircut. But the daughter will probably instead see a 'know-it-all' mother here. The appeal is relatively clear. The mother wants the daughter to go to the hairdresser. We can assume that the daughter actually understands it that way. Such a statement from the mother will cause a problem if the daughter feels patronized, takes the advice as a command, and rebels against it (see Figure 11)

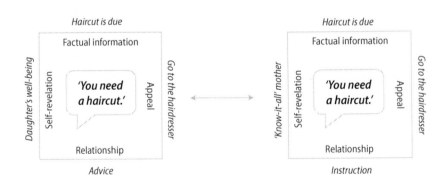

Figure 11 The four-sides model for the daughter–mother interaction

Have you experienced something similar in a communication situation within your family or at the workplace? How would you interpret your experience in light of the communication square?

INTERPRET A COMMUNICATION SITUATION USING THE FOUR-SIDES MODEL

Take any statement you have recently heard that has left you with an uneasy feeling.

- **Step 1:** Draw two squares, label each of the four sides with the four aspects of the message, and write the statement in the center of each square (similar to Figure 11). Use the left square for the sender and the right square for the receiver. (If you are used to a language that is written from the right to the left, use the right square for the sender and the left one for the receiver.)
- **Step 2:** Around each side of the sender's square, write what the sender might have meant regarding each of the four aspects.
- **Step 3:** Around each side of the receiver's square, write what the receiver might have interpreted regarding each of the four aspects.
- **Step 4:** Does what the sender (presumably) sent match what the receiver (presumably) received?
- **Step 5:** Discuss your example with your friends, colleagues, or fellow students. Can you think of any other reasonable interpretations for the individual communication situations?

You will find a template for the four-sides model on the companion website of this book at *www.econcise.com/CulturalSensitivityTraining*.

To conclude our discussion on difficult interactions, let me share a general guideline about good communication with you. If you are in a cooperative environment, you can try to achieve two goals in your communication with others:

1. Try to show appreciation by minimizing blame and maximizing praise.
2. Practice humility by minimizing praise for yourself.

But beware: this doesn't really work in competitive environments!

The 'values and development square'

While the four-sides model refers explicitly to the content of a message, the **'values and development square'** focuses more generally on how our values are related to each other. The roots of the values and development square date back to ancient times, to the Greek philosopher Aristotle. Since then, some scientists have adapted it to their own needs.

As with the four-sides model, the version of the values and development square that we will use here was also proposed by Schulz von Thun.[3] He added the 'development' part and used the square for communication situations. Since intercultural situations are predominantly communication situations, it is also suitable for our purposes.

The values and development square assumes that every human value always exists in a balance of value and counter-value, for example neat and untidy. If you take a value to the extreme, this can potentially lead to problems (in this case, either being overly tidy and fussy, or extremely untidy and chaotic).

EXAMPLE OF A VALUES AND DEVELOPMENT SQUARE FOR BEING NEAT VERSUS UNTIDY

Follow the steps below to draw a values and development square. You can compare your drawing with Figure 12 below.

Step 1: Place two rectangles next to each other with a bit of space between them. Write one value ('neat') in the left one. Write the opposite value ('untidy') in the right one. Draw two more rectangles under each of the two that you have already drawn. Label the lower left rectangle with an extreme form of 'neat' (e.g. 'fussy'), and the lower-right rectangle with an extreme form of 'untidy' (e.g. 'chaotic'). Connect the two upper rectangles with a line. In this way, you clarify that the value and counter-value are in a complementary relationship, i.e. we need them in a balanced proportion, with a good mixture of being tidy and neat. You can also connect the two lower rectangles with a line. This expresses that being fussy and being chaotic are diametrically opposed. Now you have a 'values square' in front of you.

Let us now add the 'development' aspect to the values square.

Step 2: We know that we need both values (being 'neat' and being 'untidy') in a good balance. If the left value ('neat') is exaggerated ('fussy'), however, developing in the direction of the upper-right corner ('untidy') would make sense. If you are in the lower-right corner ('chaotic'), you might want to consider developing in the direction of the upper-left corner ('neat'). Draw two directional arrows on your diagram to represent these possible development paths.

We can use the values and development square to recognize development potential for ourselves. Just be careful not to overshoot when you try to adjust (for example, then you might go from being overly fussy to completely chaotic).

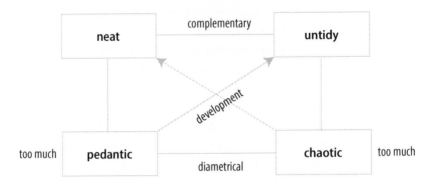

Figure 12 Values and development square for 'neat versus tidy'

EXERCISE

CREATE YOUR OWN EXAMPLE OF A
VALUES AND DEVELOPMENT SQUARE

Pick any value and create a values and development square for yourself. Maybe you hear from time to time that you are too reserved, too fidgety, or too direct? Or it always annoys you when someone is getting too emotional? If nothing comes to mind, create a values and development square for the values of stinginess versus generosity. Exchange and discuss your sketches with your friends, colleagues, or fellow students.

Dagmar Kumbier has also used **the values and development square in intercultural settings.**[4] I would like to illustrate this for you using Hall's dimension of time orientation (*monochronic* versus *polychronic*) as an example (see pp. 52-53 in Chapter 2).

Let's assume you grew up in a monochronic culture, and during an intercultural conversation a voice in your 'monochronic' head whispers to you, "Oh, they are always unpunctual!" Then you are in the lower rectangles of the values and development square as you are just seeing an extreme manifestation of polychronism.

The extreme expression of monochronism would be strict punctuality and always expecting this of others, too. This expression belongs in the other lower rectangle.

The corresponding neutral expressions, i.e. *polychronism* and *monochronism*, belong in the corresponding upper rectangles. If you now connect both top and bottom rectangles with a vertical line each, you can recognize that behind your extreme perception of 'constant unpunctuality,' there might be just a normal expression of polychronism. But since you are looking through your own cultural filter, you see an exaggeration.

You can now also connect the rectangles diagonally. Then you can see that with a monochronic view (down the diagonal line), you can be irritated by 'too much' polychronism (and maybe also accuse your communication partner of it). Looking down the diagonal line from polychronism, you could be irritated by too much monochronism.

Using the resulting graph, we can examine our own stereotypical perceptions. We can also determine in which direction we are more likely to stereotype. This is a good starting point for challenging our own perceptions, but also for preparing ourselves for meetings with people from other cultural backgrounds.

The resulting graph is not only useful for looking for potential pitfalls of a stereotypical assessment. If we look at values and their exaggerations, we can also discover the positive aspects of a value. If polychronism had no positive aspects, there would probably be no polychronic cultures.

Even though I come from a very monochronic culture and I sometimes tend to perceive a more polychronic country as 'chaotic,' when I was working in a more polychronic country I enjoyed being able to look into the offices of my colleagues at any time and clarify my concerns without first having to make an appointment. As a long-term oriented person who loves setting up detailed plans, having a 'plan B,' and taking preventive action, I learned to appreciate the attitude in a more short-term oriented country of "We will solve problems when they arise." (British people would probably phase it as "We will cross that bridge when we come to it!") I have recognized that such an attitude can actually be quite liberating, as you feel less under pressure (however, it didn't save me from falling back into my plans and precautions when I got back home).

CREATE A VALUES AND DEVELOPMENT SQUARE FOR A CULTURAL DIMENSION

- **Step 1:** Take a dimension from one of the cultural systems that we discussed in Chapter 2 and draw up a values and development square for it. The two poles of the dimension belong in the upper two rectangles.
- **Step 2:** Position yourself in the upper-right or left rectangle according to your background.
- **Step 3:** Based on the values and development square you drew in step 1 and your position from step 2, to which stereotypes could you be predisposed? How could you prevent a stereotype-based reaction in a conversation with a person who belongs to the opposite upper rectangle?
- **Step 4:** Consider how you might feel if this person were to see and treat you with their stereotypical glasses. What could be the positive aspects of the other pole of the dimension you have chosen?

Using the inner team to analyze intercultural conflict situations

In Chapter 3, we took a look at the 'inner team' (see pp. 89-94). As we discussed, it can be used to clarify your position on an issue or to prepare for an interaction. It is also a great tool for interpreting cross-cultural situations.

Remember that your inner team consists of your own individual team players, plus these four team players that are important in intercultural situations:

- the one who **represents our own culture,**
- the **culturally interested** one,
- the one who is **full of stereotypes,**
- and the one who **loves the other culture** in this particular situation.

You can gather your inner team in the aftermath of a problematic situation. What impressions and thoughts arise? Which team player felt seen, and who was overlooked? Use the inner team to carefully and calmly clarify what happened to you in that situation and why. Your team will help you to better understand how you feel about the situation.

The insights you have gained from answering the questions above are a starting point for being better prepared for future meetings. Identify those team players who came out of the situation dissatisfied. What would they have needed in the situation? Are there ways to satisfy them in a next meeting?

Try to find a mindset that is authentic to you, where all of your team players are equally satisfied. Sometimes it can be surprising what kind of creative ideas emerge when you try to balance your different, supposedly conflicting inner desires and needs.

Looking at interactions from different angles

You now have some tools at hand for analyzing difficult interactions. They should also help you to come up with solutions. You can apply these tools universally and use them to clarify any specific communication situation.

Communication situations have a few additional aspects, however, and each of them has its own pitfalls. Of course, you will not always be able to predict all the possible pitfalls. But it does make sense to look at intercultural interactions from a few different angles (see Figure 13 for an overview of some of the angles we will discuss below). This can help you to be well prepared for your intercultural encounters.

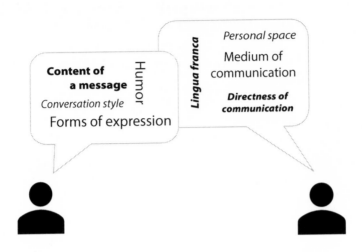

Figure 13 Selected aspects of intercultural communication

Content of the message

Of course, the content of a message is of crucial importance. Both communication partners should mentally refer to the same thing and be equally willing to exchange ideas about this matter. If an issue is more important for one of you than the other, you will pay different amounts of attention to your conversation, which can make mutual understanding more difficult.

Please remember that there are topics that are not openly discussed in certain cultures. Some issues are only talked about in private, not professionally. In some cultures, for example, there is little talk about personal sensitivities.

YOUR TABOO TOPICS

What are the topics you do not usually discuss openly in your culture, but instead only in the circle of your closest friends and family members? How do you feel when such a topic is discussed outside this close circle?

Think about how you would react when a topic which is a taboo subject for you is discussed. What would your 'inner team' say about it?

How could you recognize that you have brought up a taboo topic for other people? What could you do in such a case?

Context of the information

The **context** is the environment in which communication takes place. It makes a difference whether you are talking to your friends at a party or with your boss in a formal meeting.

Edward Hall, whose cultural system we discussed in Chapter 2, applies the term 'context' to describe the environment or circumstances in which a piece of information is embedded.[5] In some cultures, all the necessary information (about both content and the environment or circumstances in which it is embedded) is already explicitly included in the message (**low-context cultures**). In other cultures, people implicitly understand the context of a piece of information from the communication situation and the relationship between the communication partners without having to explicitly express the information about the circumstances in the message itself (**high-context cultures**).

Thus, the participants of a conversation differ in their expectations regarding the content of a message, depending on whether they are from a high- or low-context culture.

If you receive a message and feel that some things remained unsaid and that you are missing important details, then don't be afraid to ask for clarification. Your counterpart may simply come from a higher-context culture than you do.

If, on the other hand, you have the feeling that someone is just jabbering at you with excessive details, then your conversation partner might come from a lower-context culture than your own.

How can you prepare yourself for a conversation with someone with higher- or lower-context needs than yours?

Be prepared to convey more contextual information than you usually do when you meet with a communication partner who is used to a lower-context environment than you are. In this case, you will probably also receive significantly more contextual information than you are used to. Try to listen attentively, so that you do not miss the important information within the wider context.

If you meet someone who is used to a higher-context environment than your own, your conversation partner might be annoyed because you are giving them too much information to accompany the important message. Keep in mind that this is not about what you are saying, but that you are explaining too much in the eyes of your communication partner.

EXERCISE

HOW MUCH CONTEXT DO YOU NEED?

Do you prefer high-context or low-context communication? Go back to page 52 in Chapter 2 to remind yourself of your cultural profile according to Hall's cultural system.

Consider how you could react if your communication partners convey too much or too little context for you in their messages. Consult your 'inner team' about this.

Compare your need for context with your friends, colleagues, or fellow students. Are you similar or different? What might this imply if you were discussing an important topic together? Remember that similarities, as well as differences, can lead to both opportunities and risks.

How could you tell that you are providing too much or too little context for your conversation partner? How could you act if you recognize a mismatch?

Conversation style

Cultures differ in how conversations are conducted within them, and how people deal with each other in these conversations. Besides culture, it also depends on the specific situation. For example, in a family environment, conversations are conducted differently than in companies or at universities. Your conversations with friends typically differ from those with colleagues or fellow students. The type of communication behavior, which is also called the **conversation style**, can differ.

The conversation style involves, for example, the sequence in which people speak. Does everyone wait until the speaker has finished or does everyone just talk when they feel it is the right time?

Imagine that you are used to waiting for the speaker to finish. If you are taking part in a conversation where everyone talks when they feel like it, you will probably never get a chance to speak. However, if you are used to talking whenever you feel like it, but it is normal for your conversation partners to let each other finish, they may consider you to be very rude.

You can use the language which is being spoken as a very rough guideline to cultural preferences. In English, it is more common to let the other person finish before speaking. If you hear a Romance language being spoken, it is more likely that the participants in the conversation will interrupt each other. In Asia, it is more common to leave some time between contributions to the conversation. In the Arabic-speaking world, you may encounter more overlapping speech.[6]

The conversation style also includes whether pauses in speech or pauses between speakers are accepted. For some cultures, pauses mean uncertainty, and people try to avoid them. In other cultures, pauses are deliberately included to allow the speaker to reflect on what has been said.

You probably do not feel equally comfortable with all conversation styles. The next exercise will give you an opportunity to examine your preferences more closely.

YOUR PREFERRED CONVERSATION STYLE

Consider which conversation style suits you better and you feel more comfortable with. Do you interrupt others while speaking or do you wait for your turn? Can you endure silence in a conversation or not?

Compare your conversation style with that of your friends, colleagues, or fellow students. Where do you see similarities? Where do you differ from each other? What might this imply if you were discussing an important topic together? Remember that similarities, as well as differences, can lead to both opportunities and risks.

How would you feel if you were confronted with a very different conversation style? How could you react to create a situation that is comfortable for you? Consult your 'inner team' about this.

What could you do if you get the feeling that the person you are talking to is not comfortable with your conversational style?

EXERCISE

EXPERIENCE DIFFERENT CONVERSATION STYLES IN A DISCUSSION

- **Step 1:** Assign each of your friends, colleagues, or fellow students a different style of taking turns (interrupting or waiting until the other speakers have completed their thoughts or leaving some time

Forms of communication

We distinguish between verbal communication, paraverbal communication, and nonverbal communication.[7]

- **Verbal communication** includes both the spoken word and written texts.
- **Paraverbal communication** is expressed in the voice and in speech behavior. Does someone speak in a high or low voice? Does the speaker change pitch and volume or does everything sound the same? Paraverbal expression is about the way in which we speak without considering the interaction behavior (we use the term conversation styles to refer to how we speak and/or behave in interaction with others—see above).
- **Nonverbal communication** is often simply equated with body language, which certainly accounts for the largest share of nonverbal communication. However, it includes everything that is not expressed through verbal communication, for example facial expression, sighing, or your style of clothing.

Nonverbal communication usually takes place unconsciously. For example, it is very difficult to give a genuine smile on purpose, rather than as an unconscious reaction to something that you find funny or uplifting. Eye blinks and certain body reactions also occur unconsciously as micro-movements. Nevertheless, body movements can be trained, even if it is difficult to lose your automatic reactions completely.

What can differ in particular between some cultures is the **intensity of movements**. For example, in some cultures, it would be common for a lecturer to gesture or move about a lot when speaking. In other cultures, however, lecturers are more likely to stand almost motionless behind the lectern.

If you are a more reserved person, you may come across as 'boring' in more 'active' cultures. Conversely, if you come from a more active culture, you may make your listeners from a 'calmer' culture nervous.

EXERCISE

YOUR MOVEMENTS DURING PRESENTATIONS

Have you ever watched a recording of yourself giving a presentation? If not, have someone record you while you present and then watch the video. How much do you tend to move around the room? What do you do with your arms, hands, and face?

Think about how you might move less if you are an active person, and how you might move more if you are a reserved person. How would that make you feel during a presentation?

Practice displaying different levels of nonverbal 'activity' for a presentation, especially if you have to give presentations in other countries.

It is not only our body posture and facial expression that send nonverbal signals. Touching each other (or not), smells, appearance, and nonlinguistic sounds are nonverbal signals, too.

You'll already be aware that smell (such as perfume) can be used to impress someone you like. But here, too, there are differences between cultures regarding the type and intensity of scents that are preferred. To what extent our natural body odors are tolerated or not is, for example, culturally influenced. Likewise, if you don't like and don't use perfume, in a country where natural odors are undesirable (and are therefore overlaid with artificial odors), you may be unpleasantly noticed.

Appearance can also influence nonverbal communication, for example through the clothes we wear. Clothing identifies membership of social groups. It can also signal how much value we place on our appearance. There are different interpretations between cultures here, which means that there is a danger of being misjudged. Therefore, it's best to familiarize yourself with the preferences of the country and also the environment (e.g. work, school, or party) you're planning to spend time in before you are packing your bags. A few years ago, I was at a partner university in Russia with a group of German students. At the first disco evening, the German girls felt discouraged because the Russian girls had dressed up much more than them.

Even nonlinguistic sounds can be a source of difference between cultures. In which countries are you allowed to smack and slurp, and where is it frowned upon? In which countries is it even considered good manners? Intestinal sounds or burping are also accepted to different degrees in some countries.

Many of these aspects of communication, especially appearance, are known as 'dos and don'ts.' You can check them out online before you meet someone from another culture. If you already know each other, you can agree directly on the dress code (to avoid a meeting that ends up with a simple role exchange in which everyone follows the dress code of the other country).

'DOS AND DON'TS' IN YOUR OWN CULTURE

If someone asked you what clothing is appropriate in your culture in different situations, what table manners apply, and what other 'dos and don'ts' exist, how would you answer? Which manners and 'dos and don'ts' would you tell them about?

Based on your answers, develop a list of aspects you would want to consider about another country to prepare yourself before you go there.

Personal space

Personal space represents the area around a person. If another person intrudes into your personal space, you may feel uncomfortable. There are invisible boundaries around this personal space, and the size of it depends on different aspects, e.g. on age, gender, personality, the particular situation people are in, and how much people like each other. Culture also influences the size of someone's personal space.

Personal space was another aspect that Hall was interested in as a differentiating factor between cultures (see page 53 in Chapter 2).[8] Hall refers to cultures in which personal space is smaller as **public cultures,** and cultures in which personal space is larger as **private cultures**.

Private cultures strongly demarcate their property (this is the most visible characteristic of personal space). You have probably noticed bath towels on unused sun loungers on the beach, for example. In such cultures, you should be especially careful not to use personal items without asking beforehand. Don't be too surprised, on the other hand, if someone from a less private culture than yours simply sits down at your desk or drinks from your cup.

The distance that people keep from each other when they are talking is also a visible sign of personal space in a culture. Try out the following experiment with someone you know well.

PERSONAL SPACE EXPERIMENT

The next time you talk with a person you get along with well, while standing, reduce your distance a bit. It probably won't take long for the other person to take a step back. Keep doing this (as subtly as you can) and see how far you move away from your starting point. (Afterwards, don't forget to tell the other person what you were up to!)

This experiment also works the other way around (i.e. walking away from someone), but from my experience, not quite as well. If the distance between two people is too small, their personal space is violated. That means danger, which must be reacted to immediately. With too much distance, you may want to get a bit closer, but this is usually easier to bear than a violated boundary.

The exercise will probably not work so well if you do it with someone else reading this book, because they know the automatism and can consciously decide not to react as expected. But you can share your experiences with them following the exercise.

How much **physical touch** people allow or can bear is an expression of the size of personal space in a culture, too. In cultures with smaller personal spaces, hugging and touching are more common. If you prefer a larger private space, think about how you would react in advance in case your personal space is violated, for example, by someone trying to hug you. Flinging abruptly could be perceived as rejecting the other person. In a culture with larger personal spaces, however, your hugs may be perceived as crossing boundaries.

When you plan or expect to interact with other cultures, find out beforehand what their preferred personal space is like. Invading personal space that may be much larger than you expect it to be could make people uncomfortable. Keeping your distance to respect an assumed larger personal space that is actually smaller than you think, on the other hand, could be understood as a way of distancing yourself or even a type of rejection. If you come from a culture with a larger personal space, be mentally prepared for people getting too close to you. Think about how you want to react to this in advance.

EXERCISE

YOUR OWN PERSONAL SPACE

Do you have a large or a small personal space? Take a look again at how you defined your personal space in the corresponding exercise in Chapter 2 (see page 53).

Think about how you might react if the person you are talking to is getting too close to you or keeps too much distance from you. How would you feel if someone used your personal possessions when you really don't want them to? Consult your 'inner team' about this.

Compare your need for personal space with that of your friends, colleagues, or fellow students. Do you have similar needs or are they different? What might this imply if you were having a party together? Remember that similarities, as well as differences, can lead to both opportunities and risks.

How can you sense if you are getting too close to or keeping too much distance from the person you are talking to? What could you do in such a case?

Medium of communication

Most of the time, we don't think explicitly about which medium we use to communicate. We use whatever seems to make most sense in the moment. Based on our experiences and past socialization, we usually make a good choice. However, communication media differ in terms of their suitability for successful communication. Choosing a wrong medium can become a reason for miscommunication.

What options do we have for choosing the medium of communication?

The first decision to make is about whether the communication needs to happen in real time or not. Communication is (temporally) **synchronous** if the people involved respond immediately to each other. In contrast, communication is (temporally) **asynchronous** if the communication partners do not take part in the communication at the same time.

Secondly, we can consider whether we communicate **orally** or **in writing**.

These two decisions determine the choice of the communication medium.

If we want to communicate in writing and asynchronously, we can use email or a traditional letter as the medium of communication. Via an instant messaging service, we can communicate orally or in writing, and usually asynchronously. The telephone and online conferencing systems allow synchronous oral communication, and voice messages are asynchronous oral communication.

Which medium of communication is best?

Two theories address which media are particularly useful for specific types of communication situation.

Richard L. Daft and Robert H. Lengel developed the **media richness theory**.[9] The richer the medium through which the communication occurs, the theory says, the less ambiguous the communication. Following this theory, you will prefer rich media when you have to clarify complex issues. By allowing more nonverbal aspects (e.g. body language and emotional signals) to be transmitted, you can reduce ambiguity as they provide additional clues for interpreting a message. In this sense, a direct conversation in a face-to-face meeting would be preferable to a phone call or email. While the theory proves useful in practical application, it has not yet been empirically proven.

Building on the media richness theory, Alan Dennis and Joseph Valacich also considered the simultaneity of the communication and developed their **media synchronicity theory**.[10] Their basic argument is that high synchronicity reduces ambiguity.

Synchronicity is not limited to pure temporal synchronicity. It also refers to opportunities for immediate feedback, editing, and reusing messages. The more a medium offers such opportunities, the higher the synchronicity of the communication, and the lower the danger of ambiguities.

What does this mean for us in an intercultural environment? Since cultural differences increase the risk of misinterpretation, it makes sense to choose a medium with the highest possible synchronicity. Try to meet your communication partners from other cultures in person, or at least in a videoconference call. Telephone calls or voice-only chats are less promising, because there's a lack of non-verbal clues and they don't allow you to edit and reuse messages.

For written communication, it is best to use a medium in which the messages remain permanently available, such as email or a forum. An instant messaging service has less synchronicity in this respect (although it can be synchronous in time) because the messages cannot be edited or reused as easily. An instant messaging service allows even less synchronicity when you communicate via voice messages.

EXERCISE

WHICH MEDIA DO YOU USE FOR COMMUNICATION?

Can you identify patterns in which media you normally use for different types of communication? Which media do you usually use with your fellow students or work colleagues, your friends, your family, and with strangers (e.g. online)? How personal, factual, and emotional are the topics that you are discussing via the respective media?

Compare your media use with that of your friends, colleagues, or fellow students. Can you recognize any patterns between you? How does your media use differ? What might that imply if you were to work together on a project? Remember that similarities, as well as differences, can lead to both opportunities and risks.

Directness of communication

When you are talking, you can express a thought exactly as you had it in your mind. Alternatively, you can try to phrase it in such a way that it is adapted to the context of the conversation. How bluntly a thought is expressed is what we call the **directness of communication**.

With **direct communication**, people say directly what they mean. They express themselves clearly, unambiguously, and unequivocally. We mainly find direct communication in low-context cultures. The message contains all the information needed for understanding. People are not afraid to address conflicts openly.

With **indirect communication**, people paraphrase what they want to say. In particular, they hide negative content, criticism, and rejections behind hints or soften them with fuzzy expressions. We mainly find indirect communication in high-context cultures. The receiver has to infer parts of the information from the context, which lies in the communication's setting but also in knowing when a particular phrase really means something else, and what the implied meaning is. People shy away from addressing conflicts openly.

Direct and indirect communication can also be observed on the relationship level. When making explicit factual statements that are 'non-negotiable,' you are signaling that you are focused on the matter at hand and that the human aspect of the conversation is less important. In contrast, when you phrase statements in such a way that they leave some room for interpretation and negotiation, you invite interaction. In such cases, you are considering how the communication partner feels about a message and choose your words accordingly.

If you tend to speak rather cautiously, conversation partners who expect explicit statements may feel insecure, or might even think you are not very competent. If you make very confident statements, on the other hand, your communication partners might feel overlooked when they are used to statements that are negotiable and to a communication style in which the other person and their thoughts are more involved.

HOW DIRECTLY DO YOU COMMUNICATE?

Think about how directly you typically communicate. What kind of phrasing do you feel more comfortable with? Do you get straight to the point, or do you phrase things more carefully and consider how your conversation partner might perceive a statement?

Compare your notes with those of your friends, colleagues, or fellow students. Which similarities and differences do you notice? What might this imply if you were discussing an interpersonal problem together in a team situation? Remember that similarities, as well as differences, can lead to both opportunities and risks.

How would you feel if you were receiving feedback on a piece of work you completed from someone who expressed statements more directly or indirectly than you do? How could you react to create a situation that is comfortable for you? Consult your 'inner team.'

How could you proceed if you notice that the person you are talking to is not comfortable with the way you are phrasing things?

Lingua franca

When people with different native languages meet, they agree on a **common language** in which they will speak to each other. This is the **lingua franca** for that group of people. The lingua franca does not necessarily have to be English (although it often is). People will agree on a language that is best spoken by most of the group members. They might even agree on a language that is a foreign language to everyone involved.

As soon as a group uses a lingua franca, there are many sources of misunderstanding simply based on language use. We will only cover a few key points here. If you want to learn more about this topic, check out Alexandra Morgan's book *Coaching International Teams*, in which she has analyzed this widespread problem in detail.[11]

Problems with the use of a lingua franca

The biggest problem with using a lingua franca is probably the **different levels of language proficiency.** Even if everyone has a certificate of the same language level (e.g. according to the Common European Framework of Reference), you cannot be sure that everyone has an equally good command of the language in question. We often do not notice such differences directly. They will, however, become noticeable through misunderstandings.

No matter how well we master a foreign language, we cannot express our thoughts and feelings in it as well as in our native language. Nuances often remain unsaid. But it is these nuances that could make the crucial difference between superficial and real understanding. In addition, even between countries and regions that speak the same native language, the meaning of individual words can be different.

Another difficulty in using a foreign language is that there are **'false friends' between languages.** These are words that sound the same or similar, but can have drastically different meanings. For example, "irritiert sein" in German means "to wonder" in English, together with a bit of an expression of surprise. When I wrote to a colleague that I was wondering about something he did, using "to irritate" (which is more like "being annoyed"), our communication went directly off track. After checking the dictionary, I wrote a detailed explanation and included a profound apology, which fortunately put everything back on track again.

We can express ourselves more accurately in our native language and can describe details more clearly. Words are easier to find, and speech is more fluent. To find this flow in a foreign language requires an extremely high level of language competence.

Possible effects when using a lingua franca

If we are not native speakers of the lingua franca, we often do not find the right words in the foreign language right away. Maybe we are also not able to form sentences as quickly as we would want to. This can set us at a disadvantage and hinder us from fully taking part in team discussions. Maybe we cannot express or articulate all of our ideas in adequate detail.

Thus, we might not be able to contribute to a group task to our full potential. Others may even perceive us as being less competent.

Language is always an expression of culture and identity too. Some people also feel less motivated to use an unfamiliar language. They may feel that they cannot express themselves sufficiently, and that they are not sufficiently understood. This can lead to a diminished commitment to the group work, frustration, and disappointment.

What can you do about it?

The most important point is probably to be aware of the problems that can arise with the use of a lingua franca. You can try to develop a **sensitivity to these problems**. This is especially important for those whose native language is the lingua franca.

Active listening can be very useful in conversations conducted in a lingua franca. Use questions to check whether you have understood correctly what your partners said. This ability to listen actively through asking questions is a very useful skill in general. In a lingua franca conversation, it can help to prevent misunderstandings.

You can also try to **use a language which is a foreign language for everyone involved as a lingua franca**. This may sound paradoxical because you might lose the linguistic competence of the native speakers. However, you can also potentially gain a more balanced language competence among all participants. This will also help to avoid inadvertently equating lower language competence with low professional competence.

In *Coaching International Teams*, Alexandra Morgan suggests a lot of exercises that can help members of a team to deal with the problems of using a lingua franca.[12] Here are two additional exercises that will develop your sensitivity to this aspect of communication in general.

YOU AND YOUR LINGUA FRANCA

- **Part 1:** Think about a situation where the lingua franca used was not your native language. Which of the difficulties mentioned above did you notice? Were there other things that did not go so well? How did you feel about them? What would you have needed from the native speakers to feel more comfortable?
- **Part 2:** Now think of a situation in which the lingua franca used was your native language. Could there have been situations in which your communication partners felt uncomfortable? Did you notice them? What could you do to recognize such situations more quickly and confidently? How could you support your partners in such circumstances?
- **Part 3:** Exchange ideas with your friends, colleagues, or fellow students. Discuss how you could expand your range of responses that you could use in a lingua franca setting. If you speak different languages, try using a language other than your usual one as a lingua franca in your group and find out how you feel doing so.

COMPARE YOUR ABILITY TO EXPRESS YOURSELF USING YOUR NATIVE AND YOUR FOREIGN LANGUAGES

Think about something you experienced today. Describe the situation in writing and how you felt about it: (a) in your native language, (b) in your first foreign language and (c) in your second foreign language (if possible). Give yourself two minutes for each language.

Compare your descriptions. How do they vary in length, word choice, and the amount of details you were able to cover?

The role of humor

Last but not least, a few words about the use of humor in intercultural encounters based on the work of Rod Martin, a Canadian academic who is engaged in humor research.[13]

Humor always takes place in a specific social context. When we hear a joke, we are processing it in our brain. This leads to an emotional reaction, which is usually expressed through laughter. In most cases, we want to induce a positive feeling through our humor. However, this is not guaranteed. A joke may well backfire, especially if the social context is not appropriate. Beware that **jokes are culturally bound** and might not be understood in another cultural context. Additionally, everyone also has a very personal style of humor, which does not always match with the style of our communication partners.

Therefore, we should **use humor wisely**. This is even more true in intercultural situations or when a lingua franca is used. You have probably experienced situations where your humor came across differently than intended. You have also probably noticed that people use different styles of humor for different purposes.

A little humor can contribute to a good relationship. It can also promote group cohesion. To this end, we tell jokes, and when everyone laughs, a sense of unity can emerge. Humor of this type is borne of goodwill. It is not hostile. Martin calls this type of humor an **affiliated style of humor** or benevolent humor.[14]

Some people can laugh at themselves even in difficult personal situations. They use a **self-enhancing style of humor** to better deal with stress and quickly overcome unpleasant moments.

When someone uses an **aggressive style of humor**, they are making fun of others and mocking them. Sometimes they threaten or manipulate the other person with their aggressive humor. Such behavior harms the group atmosphere and can even cause conflicts or create divisions within the group. We can easily recognize aggressive humor because those who are in the joke cannot laugh at it.

Some sufferers respond to aggressive humor with a **self-defeating style of humor**. They let others make jokes about themselves and pretend that they consider it funny. Very close to self-defeating humor is **self-depreci-**

ating humor. You make jokes about yourself to entertain others or to help them to cope with a difficult situation.

HUMOR THAT IS NOT FOR YOU

- **Part 1:** Think of a situation where someone in your group used humor, but you really didn't find it funny. Why couldn't you laugh at the joke? What style of humor did the person use? Were there cultural aspects that caused you to not be able to take the joke? How did you feel about it? How did you react, or how would you have wanted to react? If the humor was benevolent, what would you have wanted the person who was trying to be humorous to do differently?

- **Part 2:** Think of a situation in which you used friendly humor, but someone in your group really didn't find it funny. Did you consciously notice that not everyone could laugh at your joke? What could you do to recognize such situations more quickly and confidently? How could you react in such situations? If you have never been in this situation before, try to imagine it as a thought experiment.

- **Part 3:** As always, exchange ideas with your friends, colleagues, or fellow students. You could try to create a situation together where some of you don't understand each other's benevolent humor and observe how each of you is dealing with it. The main point is to expand your range of possible responses for dealing with such a situation.

YOUR STYLE OF HUMOR

Think about how strongly you tend to use the different styles of humor. At *https://www.psytoolkit.org/survey-library/humor-hsq.html* (available at the time of writing) you can find a questionnaire that helps you determine your inclination toward the different styles of humor. Use the link "Click here to run a demo of the survey" to access the questionnaire.

If you notice you often use the aggressive and/or self-defeating styles of humor, try to practice using the benevolent and self-enhancing styles of humor more often, so that you can use humor in intercultural situations that is less likely to cause friction or division.

Some general hints for effective intercultural communication

This book has armed you with many suggestions for how to prepare for intercultural situations, how to solve difficulties that arise, and how to analyze such situations afterwards. Perhaps you are wondering whether there are some more general tips for intercultural communication, especially for situations where you do not know in advance which people you will meet.

Below I will provide a few general hints for effective communication in an intercultural context, which also summarizes some of the ideas that we have discussed in this chapter.

Mutual respect

Mutual respect is probably **the most important building block of successful interpersonal communication**, especially in an intercultural context. Respect your communication partners as equal individuals with equal rights. Accept that although people are basically the same, they can be very different in their individual characteristics, desires, and behaviors. There is nothing inherently 'good' or 'bad' about these differences—it is just the way it is. Let yourself **be inspired by the differences**, recognize them as enriching, and try to find creative solutions for your joint tasks together.

You can express respect in different ways. One of them is culturally appropriate eye contact. Through your posture, you can signal friendliness or withdrawal. And your voice can sound benevolent or aggressive, too.

Respect is closely linked with your **inner attitude**. Remind yourself again and again what it means to treat each other with respect. This will help you respond to your conversation partners in a non-judgmental way. Remember that your own knowledge, perceptions, and beliefs are only appropriate and valid in your own individual context. All other people have their own individual context with their own knowledge, perceptions, and beliefs, too.

Be open to taking on roles or displaying behaviors that are appropriate to the specific situation. In this way, you can strengthen group cohesion and support group communication. Sometimes it might be appropriate to act more 'open' and at other times more reserved. In some discussions you may need to act as a moderator, while in others it might be more important that you contribute ideas. Sometimes, being provocative is helpful, while at other times, it will be better to promote harmony.

Strategies for coping with crises

When you notice that an intercultural communication situation is turning into a **crisis situation**, there are three steps to consider:

1. reflect on your own situation,
2. analyze the situation, and
3. prepare for collaboration.

Prior learnings and exercises from this book should help you to answer these questions. The section entitled "A general framework for analyzing difficult interaction" (pp. 101-104), as well as the 'communication square' (pp. 104-107) and the 'values and development square' (pp. 108-112), can support you with your reflection and analysis tasks. And don't forget your 'inner team,' which can provide you with insights for all three of these steps.

Be sensitive to how what you want to say might be received by your conversation partners. You may have already conducted some exercises together with your friends, colleagues, or fellow students as you've worked through this book (e.g. the 'four-sides model' exercise on p. 107, or the lingua franca exercise on p. 131). Maybe you have noticed that you could not get across what you wanted to say. In this type of situation, you might try to **emphasize the important thoughts** you want to get across again.

In general, you can **repeat** what you have said. It can sometimes be helpful if you use different wording than before. Additionally, you can **ask your listeners how they interpreted or understood** what you have said. When planning how to convey your message, especially when using a lingua franca, you could consider incorporating these tactics, for example by building repetition into your communication.

Using communication to solve communication problems can be very helpful. This is called **meta-communication** (see below). This can help to uncover reasons for unsuccessful communication and avoid it in the future.

Let me make a note of caution here, however. Adapting or restraining your own communication style in a way that does not feel natural can potentially extinguish the vitality of the interaction. The participants in the communication situation might also behave in an over-adapted and therefore no longer authentic way. In that case, nobody will enjoy the communication anymore, leading to less than optimal results.

I would also like to warn you once again of the stereotypes that lie slumbering within all of us. Differences are neither 'good' nor 'bad.' They should not be a reason for demonizing another person. Remember that you appear to be just as different in your counterparts' eyes as they appear to yours.

Meta-communication

Meta-communication, that is communicating about the communication, can start before the actual cooperation or conversation begins. You can try to anticipate the most critical situations and consider preventive measures. You could, for example, define communication rules for the group or just for a specific discussion. Thus, you will not only talk about the communication process and the way you talk to each other, but also about the relationships between the communication partners.

There are a few guidelines to follow for successful meta-communication. Arguably the most important one is to strive for a **benevolent atmosphere** in which everyone feels seen, heard, and accepted (including their emotions and fears).

You can also talk about feelings, needs, and expectations. Focus on what you actually perceive and do not start interpreting the behavior of others or ascribe intentions to this behavior. Accept what others say just as you want them to accept what you say. The point is to try to **understand each other's truth**, thus achieving mutual understanding.

Ideally, all parties involved should be willing to communicate and clarify the difficulties. This includes acknowledging when there is a conflict. Examine your own goals in this conflict. Do you perhaps have less conscious goals that influence your behavior nonetheless? If in doubt, ask your 'inner team' about this specific communication situation.

I hope that after having read these first four chapters, you will now feel ready to confidently face intercultural communication situations. However, to take your skills one level further, take a look at Chapter 5, where you will get an overview of other areas in which intercultural sensitivity can be very helpful too. In addition, I will also help you to create a plan for developing your intercultural competencies to a higher level.

KEY TAKEAWAYS FROM CHAPTER 4

1. **Appreciating people from other cultures** as equals (as equally valuable human beings) is the basis for getting along well with each other.

2. A first step to solving critical intercultural problems is the **analysis of the underlying cultural orientations and value systems** of the people involved.

3. Different **communication styles** (e.g. directly or indirectly addressing critical issues) can lead to misunderstandings and disagreements.

4. Different cultural backgrounds can lead to words and/or sentences being understood differently from what the speaker intended. The **'four-sides model'** can help you to recognize such misunderstandings.

5. If different value systems seem to clash, the **'values and development square'** can help you recognize the positive aspects of the supposedly opposing attitudes, and to include them in your own scheme of thought and action.

6. The more aware you are of what can go wrong in communication, and the better you can prepare for it in advance, the better you will be able to **handle unexpected situations**. Your 'inner team' can help you to be well prepared.

Notes for Chapter 4

1   Nerdinger (2012).
2   Schulz von Thun (1981).
3   Ibid.
4   Kumbier (2006).
5   Hall (1982).
6   Trompenaars and Hampden-Turner (1998).
7   Deresky (2016).
8   Hall (1973).
9   Draft and Lengel (1983).
10 Dennis and Valacich (1999).
11 Morgan (2022).
12 Ibid.
13 Martin (2006).
14 Ibid.

5

Reach out: Taking your intercultural competence to the next level

This chapter enables you to:

» Assess your intercultural sensitivity according to the developmental model of intercultural sensitivity (DMIS).
» Identify possibilities for developing your cultural sensitivity.
» Plan and start to implement concrete steps for taking your cultural sensitivity to the next level.

We have almost reached the end of our excursion into intercultural sensitivity. But this book wouldn't be complete without some hints on how to continue your journey in this field.

In this chapter, I will first introduce a few ways of **self-assessing your current level of intercultural sensitivity.** This will help you determine where you are at the moment, and where you want to go from here.

After that, we will take a look at what **intercultural competence** includes beyond intercultural sensitivity. I will also give you some advice about different types of intercultural training programs, thus enabling you to find the right training program for you.

You will probably already have an idea about how you would like to shape your future career and life. Later in this chapter, we will address a few topics that might be important in your future career (including **cultural shock, the mindset of leaders, negotiation, and dealing with conflicts**). I will also give you some basic information and tips about which intercultural competencies could be of particular interest in these areas. If one of these areas is important for you, you can immediately assess which competencies you could—and should—acquire to act confidently and successfully in the respective domain.

Mark the passages that you find interesting or write down the things that you find helpful. At the end of the chapter, I will present a few **concrete steps you can take to develop your intercultural sensitivity to a higher level**. Based on this, I will invite you to draw up **your own development plan**. Use your notes to define concrete steps for your further intercultural development—and get ready to continue the journey on your own.

But let us first take stock and look at how far your intercultural sensitivity has already developed.

Intercultural sensitivity and awareness

The developmental model of intercultural sensitivity

The American sociologist **Milton Bennett** was among the first to take a more 'universal' view on intercultural competence and developing sensitivity of other cultures in general, beyond the ability to competently interact with people from other specific countries.[1] He established a model to classify the skills needed to deal with differences between cultures. This model (known as the **developmental model of intercultural sensitivity** or **DMIS** model) sees a gradual progression from stage one, where cultural differences are completely denied, to stage six, where you are able to move back and forth between cultures quite freely.

Bennett postulates that it is possible to develop from the first to the sixth stage, and describes the cognitive steps that are necessary for this development. Let us now take a closer look at each of these stages, and how you can get from one stage to the next.[2]

Stage 1: Denial of difference

At this level, people **do not recognize differences between cultures or deliberately deny these differences**. There may be several reasons for this (we discussed some of them in Chapter 1). Usually, denial of other cultures goes hand in hand with people considering their own culture to be the only 'correct' and 'true' culture. They want to have and keep the feeling that they live in a homogeneous group. Differences are perceived as being uncomfortable and undesirable.

Sometimes, people at this stage perceive other cultures in a simplified or undifferentiated way. When people in the first stage are confronted with cultural differences, they may react aggressively to fight off the recognition of the differences. In this way, they try to preserve and protect their own view.

Many people remain in the first stage because they have not had the opportunity to really encounter other cultures. It is this direct contact with people from other cultures that can help people to perceive differences and develop an awareness of the fact that there are differences between cultures. This is the most important prerequisite for transitioning to stage 2.

Stage 2: Defense against difference

When people move from stage 1 to stage 2, they are **able to perceive and accept cultural differences**. They often make a clear division between 'my culture' and the 'culture of others'. This is closely related to the phenomenon we discussed in Chapter 1 of behaving according to your own group norms and upholding an 'us versus them' attitude. One's own culture is perceived as superior, as the only 'right' one, and as the better way to live.

With such an attitude, consciously noticing cultural differences can induce people to react aggressively because they experience it as an attack on their own culture. They might also fall back on their simplistic and either romanticizing or degrading stereotypes to describe and evaluate others. People at this level sometimes belittle other cultures or feel that their culture is superior to other cultures.

If people at this level live in another country, they sometimes completely adopt the culture of the new country without reflection. Within the new culture, they may then even feel superior to their original culture.

A major reason why people remain at this second level is that they have no way of dissolving their stereotypical prejudices. Conscious encounters with people from other cultures, exchanges about similarities and differences between cultures, and a demonstration of the benefits of both similarities and differences can help us move to the third stage.

Stage 3: Minimization of difference

People at this level emphasize the **similarities between cultures**. Although they certainly perceive differences, for example, in rituals, clothing, or eating habits, they focus on the needs that human beings have in common, such as the need for food and physical safety.

However, they regard their own culture as a 'standard' and feel that their own values are (or should be) universally valid. They take their own standards of evaluation and behavior as the basis of successful interactions.

People at this level are not aware of how their cultural background influences their own actions and evaluations, and thus also their intercultural communication. For this reason, they often overestimate their own ability to be tolerant of cultural differences.

At this level, we find two basic orientations of how people overestimate the commonalities between cultures. On the one hand, there are **biological commonalities** such as eating, drinking, reproducing, and dying, which underlie our lives across cultures. On the other hand, there are universal **inner values** (e.g. health, pleasure, safety) that unite us as human beings. One danger at this level is that cultural differences can either be trivialized or romanticized by overemphasizing commonalities.

One reason for this overemphasis of commonalities could be that we are repeatedly warned against overemphasizing differences, falling into stereotypes, and devaluing other cultures. A common reaction to this is to overemphasize commonalities. For the transition to the fourth stage, it is helpful to deal with the differences between cultures consciously and recognize the potential that can lie in these differences.

Stage 4: Acceptance of difference

When people **accept differences between cultures**, they understand that socialization influences the development of their own values and norms, and thus also their own culture.

They also recognize that other people organize their lives differently and have different values (although they do not necessarily always welcome them).

People at the fourth level also understand that their culture affects how they act, behave, value, and evaluate. They see differences in behavior values, and evaluations between cultures, and can interpret their observations as differences.

Often, people at this level ask questions that reflect their genuine interest in understanding other cultures in more depth. They do not just look for information that confirms their own stereotypes, but want to really get to know people from other cultures and enter into a direct exchange with them.

At the fourth level, people respect differences and understand that norms, values, beliefs, and behaviors develop in a cultural context. The deeper you immerse yourself in other cultures, explore them, and experience real encounters, the closer you approach the fifth stage.

Stage 5: Adaptation to difference

At this stage, people change their perspective on other cultures. Other values, attitudes, and behaviors are allowed to stand on the same level as their own. **Empathy** for people of the other culture and the effective use of well-understood differences enable **successful intercultural communication**.

Empathy no longer works only for a very specific culture, but across cultures. Thus, people at the fifth level can adequately act and interact in a wide variety of communication situations. Based on empathy, they are able to behave in ways that are understood by others as intended.

People at the fifth level can consciously adjust to differences between cultures. They know that they must also understand these differences against the background and worldview of the respective cultures.

To move from the fifth to the sixth stage, people further deepen their capacity for empathy so that they can use it not only in a distinct interaction, but more generally as their 'way of life.'

Stage 6: Integration of difference

Because of their high empathic ability, people at level six appear to be 'fluent' in navigating different cultures. They can effortlessly switch between different worldviews.

Their culture is no longer a centrally determining aspect of their self-image. They see themselves as builders of their own reality and feel at home in many (if not in all) cultures. We could even say that they 'belong' to different cultures.

At the same time, people at level six are well aware that different cultures evaluate and interpret situations in different ways. They also know they can consciously choose between these different ways of evaluating and interpreting.

EXERCISE

HOW WELL DEVELOPED IS YOUR INTERCULTURAL SENSITIVITY ACCORDING TO THE DMIS MODEL?

Take some time to read the descriptions of the six levels of intercultural sensitivity according to Milton Bennett once again. Which level would you assign yourself to? What would be necessary for you to reach the next level?

Keep this in mind while reading the rest of this chapter and make notes if you get ideas for concrete steps you can take to develop your intercultural sensitivity. Then incorporate these steps into a personal development plan (which we will discuss in the last part of this chapter).

HOW HAS YOUR INTERCULTURAL SENSITIVITY ALREADY CHANGED BECAUSE OF THIS BOOK?

Discuss with your friends, colleagues, or fellow students which exercises in this book address which stages of the DMIS model.

Can you determine to what extent your own intercultural sensitivity has developed during the course of reading this book and completing the exercises? If you have worked through this book alongside others, discuss this and give each other feedback as objectively as possible.

Intercultural sensitivity as part of intercultural competence

In Chapter 1, we briefly mentioned what **intercultural competence** is all about (see pp. 23-24). You may remember that it includes **cognitive, behavioral, and affective aspects**. When you plan to take action to develop your intercultural competence to a higher level, try to focus on all three of these aspects in equal measure:

- **Cognitive (or knowledge) aspects** include everything you can know about cultures, cultural systems, the history of cultures, rituals, and customs, as well as dos and don'ts of particular cultures (see Chapter 2).
- **Behavioral aspects** mainly concern actual communication behavior when you are dealing with people from other cultures, including how you react to other people, the extent to which you use appropriate communication styles, and the extent to which you have and are able to apply strategies for resolving critical communication situations (see Chapter 4).
- **Affective (or emotional) aspects** include whether you are able to relate to people from other cultures empathically and tolerate the differences. But it is also about whether you are fundamentally interested in other cultures, how you feel in intercultural situations,

and how you are able to deal with these feelings in a productive way (see Chapters 3 and 4).

Behavioral and emotional aspects were the focus of the exercises in this book whenever I asked you to compare yourself with your friends, colleagues, or fellow students. Sometimes, the exercises directly asked you to think about how you would *behave* if you were in a certain situation, and other exercises invited you to think about how you would *feel* in such a situation.

Behavioral and emotional aspects are best practiced in direct contact with people from other cultures. The exercises in this book can give you some clues on how you could then reflect on your experiences in a meaningful and effective way.

If you want to set goals to develop the behavioral and emotional aspects of your intercultural competence, always think about including a **reflection phase** to consolidate your learnings after an intercultural experience.

The affective aspects of intercultural competence are closely related to **emotional intelligence**. In contrast to general intelligence, emotional intelligence describes how we are able to deal with our feelings. It essentially involves three skills:[3]

- First, you must be able to recognize feelings in yourself and others ('**emotion perception sensitivity**').
- Then it is a matter of distinguishing which of the observed feelings are your own and which are associated with other people ('**emotion discrimination competence**').
- Last but not least, you can then behave appropriately based on the observed feelings ('**emotion regulation competence**').

Depending on how strongly you have already developed these three skills, you might include **strengthening your emotional intelligence** in your development plan.

Types of intercultural training

Depending on how and why you would like to develop your intercultural skills, it may make sense to attend a formal **intercultural training pro-**

gram. Before deciding to participate in such a program, take a close look at what it includes and whether it fits your goals.

Intercultural training can be either **culturally universal** or **culture-specific**. This book is culturally universal because you have learned skills that can help you equally in all cultures. Culture-specific training prepares you specifically for dealing with people of one particular culture or a narrowly defined set of cultures. If you plan to live in another country, such training could be very useful preparation.

Intercultural training can be either **cognitive/trainer-oriented** or **experiential**.[4] This book attempts to combine both approaches. It is cognitive/trainer-oriented in the sense that I am trying to convey knowledge through the text of this book. But it is also experiential, because the exercises encourage you to practice things together with your friends, colleagues, or fellow students while interacting with them.

Let us have a look at other methods that are used in intercultural training:

- *Cognitive/trainer-oriented, culturally universal training* will typically include information about **cultural theories** and describe general **characteristics of intercultural behavior**.
- *Cognitive/trainer-oriented, culture-specific training* often works with **intercultural case studies** of the target culture and with analyses of certain aspects of the target culture. It may also include **culture assimilators**: a training format in which you are invited to assess descriptions of interactions with the target culture.
- *Experience-based, culturally universal training* immerses you in fictional situations of different cultural contexts using **simulations** and **role-plays**.
- *Experience-based, culture-specific training* attempts to bring learners into **direct contact with people from the target culture**. They might even try to provoke conflict situations in order to practice appropriate behavior.

In most training programs, you will find a mix of these elements. Consider to what extent the overall program can meet your expectations.

In companies, intercultural training can also take place in the form of **intercultural coaching and mediation** or special **team-building exercises**.

If you work or study in a very diverse environment, you actually experience intercultural training every day. That's where the exercises in this book can be highly useful—try to use these exercises to reflect on your day-to-day intercultural encounters, and particularly to consider any critical situations you experience. Reflect on how you could do things differently in similar situations in the future.

EXERCISE

WHAT KIND OF INTERCULTURAL TRAINING IS USED IN YOUR COURSE?

If you are currently taking part in a course that includes the development of intercultural competence (e.g. as part of a study program), consider which of the above-mentioned elements of intercultural training are implemented in this course.

Your network of contacts as a daily training ground

You can practice some intercultural skills quite easily if you **consider every encounter with another person as a training ground for interpersonal competence**. The more people from different backgrounds you know and meet, the more you can practice intercultural competence.

Have you ever thought about the cultural characteristics of people who you are close to or in regular contact with—not only in terms of national culture, but also in terms of their membership in very different groups? The more heterogeneous your contacts are, the more opportunities you will have to practice intercultural sensitivity in your everyday life. Take a fresh look at your existing network of contacts—you will be surprised by how much cultural difference you find in it.[5]

HOW DIVERSE ARE YOUR CONTACTS?

- **Step 1:** In one column, make a list of all the people you meet at least once in a while. This doesn't mean everyone who is following you on your blog or social media profile. The list should only include those with whom you interact individually.
- **Step 2:** Next to each person's name, add their gender in a second column and their age group in a third. In a fourth column, note which country this person feels affiliated to. This does not necessarily have to be the country in which this person was born or in which they currently live. If you are unsure, then consider asking them about this when you next meet. You can add more information that you consider relevant about your contacts in additional columns, for example, their job role, education, or main fields of expertise (you can also return to pp. 12-16 in Chapter 1 and see what aspects were listed there regarding culture, or to p. 64 in the final part of Chapter 2 where we addressed your cultural repository).
- **Step 3:** Evaluate your list of contacts. How diverse are they? Are different age groups represented? Do your contacts come from different countries? Where would you maybe need additional contacts to make your list more diverse? Take a note of this last one and add a corresponding activity to your development plan (see below).

Your network of contacts can help you to develop your intercultural sensitivity. Try to keep your network alive. Meet people you haven't met for a while, especially those who differ greatly from the people you have seen recently.

Another way of bringing more diversity into your network is to make sure that it doesn't include too many people who are in contact with each other. For example, if you only have colleagues from your office in your network, your contacts rarely extend very far out into the world. A network where everyone is in contact with each other runs into the danger of becoming 'incestuous.' If you sense that this is the case, try to add new contacts to your network.

Meeting new people is actually quite easy. If you are a student, then clubs, groups or parties are a great place to make new acquaintances. Besides that, how about taking a course that is not in your field of study? You can also meet new people through volunteer work. Just dare to step out of your comfort zone a bit! If you find it difficult to approach and meet new people, add concrete steps to do so in your personal development plan.

Developing your intercultural sensitivity to a higher level

Having considered the basic areas of intercultural competence in which you could identify potential for developing yourself, we will now deal with some specific areas for enhancing your intercultural sensitivity. For your own personal development program, try to select the areas that you consider most important (at least at the moment) for your own journey through life.

Culture shock

If you plan to live in another country for an extended period of time and you are not yet familiar with its culture, you may experience what is called 'culture shock.'[6]

Culture shock typically comes in **five stages:**[7]

1. It usually starts with being quite euphoric about the upcoming adventure and looking forward to the many experiences ahead. Everything seems new, 'exotic,' and positive. Maybe the dreams that you have associated with the trip will come true. At this early stage, you will predominantly perceive the positive sides of the new culture. This is the **honeymoon phase**.

2. You then try to settle in this unfamiliar country, looking for accommodation, a new job, schooling for your children, etc. Not everything goes as smoothly as planned. There might be misunderstandings about some things, which you can't avoid despite good

preparation. But since you assume that you have not prepared well enough, you often blame yourself for these misunderstandings. This is the **rejection phase**.

3. To better endure the emotional stress of not being understood, you may try to surround yourself with people from your own culture. That's one way to find relief in an environment that is perceived as difficult and maybe even rejecting. Sometimes, the feeling can arise that others are to blame for the misunderstandings. This leads to a revaluation of your own culture. We are in the middle of the **crisis phase**.

4. After the first bitter disappointments, you are ready to deal with the misunderstandings in a more constructive way. You start to accept the differences, endure the contradictions, and strive for understanding. This brings us to the **recovery phase**.

5. This will open the path to understanding the differences. This can go as far as adopting the behavior of the new culture. You might also find solutions and combine ideas from both cultures meaningfully. This is the **adjustment phase**.

The process of culture shock will take you on an emotional roller-coaster ride from euphoria to frustration to satisfaction. Stereotypical thinking will change into culturally purposeful thinking, and your self-image will expand from being nationally shaped to becoming globally shaped.

If you look at the processes that take place during culture shock, you will certainly recognize some parallels to the development of intercultural sensitivity according to Bennett. Strengthening your intercultural sensitivity is therefore an important goal in the preparation for a longer stay abroad, as it can cushion the effects of culture shock.

There are other things you can do to **diminish the effects of culture shock**, too. It always makes sense to familiarize yourself with the culture of your destination country as much as possible in advance. Knowing the language of the destination country can certainly be very helpful too. This will make it easier to interact with the locals, and everyday life will become much easier. Try to integrate into the society of your host country as soon as possible—that's the best way to learn how to communicate effectively with local people.

Keep in close contact with your family and friends, regardless of whether they have stayed behind in your home country or are traveling with you. You might think that this could distract you from acclimatizing to the new culture (and maybe it does). But in difficult times, when you are unable to understand others or you feel misunderstood, family and friends can give you the support that you desperately need.

Last but not least, try to be kind to yourself. Allow yourself breaks and get enough rest. A cultural change requires a lot of energy.

Before you return from your stay abroad, be mentally prepared to experience **reverse culture shock**. That's when you will have to get used to your home culture again.

Leadership in an intercultural environment

Leadership is a challenging job in itself, but it can be even more challenging when you have to lead intercultural teams. Many researchers have dealt with the topic, and it seems that success in **leading intercultural teams** depends, in particular, on adopting an appropriate mindset.[8]

Let's take a look at two completely different sources that explain the foundational elements of this mindset. Maybe you will find some ideas for the development of your own intercultural sensitivity here, which you can then incorporate into your personal development plan (see below in this chapter). This would be especially useful if you plan to lead intercultural teams (or if you already do so).

Gary P. Ferraro, an American researcher of applied anthropology and intercultural communication, tried to identify general characteristics of good leaders. He distinguishes between your own working style and a general attitude:[9]

- Regarding **your own working style**, he emphasizes openness and flexibility. It is important to be a good team player. It is also very helpful if you can reconcile global and local goals, and then implement them using local practices. It probably goes without saying that you should be able to manage intercultural communication situations well.
- Regarding the **general attitude**, Ferraro emphasizes that it is important to keep the entire system (i.e. all involved people, the organi-

zational culture, relationships to other departments etc.) and its complex interactions in mind. You should be able to operate well in intercultural and interdisciplinary environments. You should not be frightened by changes, but see them as opportunities for improvement. New encounters in unfamiliar environments should stimulate your joy of learning, as you ideally see them as an opportunity for both professional and personal development.

In the GLOBE Study, which we first encountered in Chapter 2 (see pp. 45-47), House et al. examined requirements for (intercultural) leaders in more detail.[9] According to that study, the **most important leadership skills** are:

- *leading in a team-oriented manner, building effective teams,* and *setting a team goal,* and
- *communicating a vision and values,* as well as *placing trust in employees.*

However, the study found **differences between cultures** in the perception of these skills.

House et al. further categorized **leadership characteristics** into helpful and harmful ones:[10]

- **Helpful leadership characteristics** include those that are generally associated with good leadership (i.e. what employees typically expect from their leaders). Leaders should be trustworthy, honest, and fair. They should encourage and motivate employees and keep their eyes on the big picture. They should be able to make intelligent decisions. And last but not least, a leader must be able to build a team effectively and communicate with employees, as well as coordinate their work.
- The second category contains **harmful leadership characteristics**. People who are self-centered, uncooperative, inconsiderate, antisocial, and aloof are unlikely to become good leaders. People who are dictatorial or irritable are also not likely to be accepted as leaders.

YOUR OWN LEADERSHIP STYLE

- **Step 1:** Regardless of whether you are currently in a leadership role or not, think about the attitude that you (would) hold as a leader toward your employees, their motivation, and how well they perform at work. Write down the most important points.
- **Step 2:** To what extent does your attitude correspond to the leadership characteristics above that have been described as helpful for intercultural environments? Are there areas where you would like to develop further? (In this case, make a note and add a corresponding activity to your development plan.)
- **Step 3:** Discuss your assessment of your own attitude with your friends, colleagues, or fellow students. Are your attitudes helpful for leading in an intercultural context?

You can complete this exercise even if you don't have any leadership experience yet. In this case, think about team situations in school or college. What role did you play in the team and why? If you were not the team leader, how did you want the team leader to act? Would you be able to meet your own requirements for a 'good' leader?

Negotiations in an intercultural environment

Negotiations between people with similar cultural backgrounds are often challenging (and fail often too). You can imagine how different cultural backgrounds further complicate successful negotiation.

Helen Deresky addresses **cultural factors that influence negotiations:**[11]

- First, culture may influence the **negotiation goals**. Is the negotiation more about principles or about details? Does the focus lie on the goal of the negotiation or more on the personal relationships between the negotiating parties?

- Culture also influences **who is a member of the negotiation team and how much team members prepare for the negotiation**.
- The questions of **how much trust** there is between the negotiating partners and whether trust plays a role in concluding a contract are also culturally influenced. In some cultures, trust depends on the length and intensity of the existing relationship.

These cultural differences can lead to very different negotiation styles. Negotiations can be fact-oriented, or they can focus on the person or on underlying principles. In terms of negotiation behavior, we find defensive, aggressive, and trusting patterns. Depending on the cultural background, we may face deception and pressure, but also trusting relationships.

As you already know from Chapter 4 (see p. 119), you can also expect to see differences in verbal and nonverbal behavior. We should also be prepared for our negotiating partners to either be late or not tolerate our own lateness.

Jean-Claude Usunier, a French honorary professor of marketing, studied different negotiation concepts in different cultures and assigned them to three culture-specific aspects of negotiation.[12] (You will notice certain parallels between the negotiation concepts and cultural dimensions from Chapter 2.) This may provide you with some initial guidance on how to prepare yourself for negotiations in other counties or with people from other cultures.

The three **culture-specific aspects of negotiation** are:

1. **The behavioral preferences of the negotiating partners.** This includes a person's interpersonal orientation, which can range from self-interest to a desire for harmony. Power always plays a key role here (ranging from formalized power to informal influence). Behavioral preferences also include the willingness to take risks. How much uncertainty can the negotiating partners tolerate? Are decisions made by a single person who is present, by a more senior person who is not part of the immediate negotiation team, or through a unified team decision?
2. **Underlying negotiation concepts.** Is trust or mistrust the basis of the negotiation? What is the basic understanding of negotiation among the parties involved? A negotiation can be a logical process

with a clear end. However, some cultures understand negotiation as an ongoing dialogue.

3. **The negotiation process itself.** This includes the negotiating style. Are the parties clearly focused on specific goals, or is it more a matter of following basic principles? This third aspect also considers the results which are achieved with the negotiation. Some cultures prefer a clearly defined contract, and others less explicit agreements.

Within this context, Stephen E. Weiss, a professor of policy and international business, suggests five approaches to negotiating in a cross-cultural environment.[13] Which of those approaches you should choose depends on how familiar you and your negotiating partners are with each other's culture (please note that these approaches work much better in cooperative environments rather than competitive environments):[14]

- If **both sides are only slightly familiar with the other culture**, Weiss advises bringing in a moderator for the negotiation.
- If **one of the two sides is familiar with the other's culture**, but the other side is not, there are two approaches: (a) the knowledgeable side should adapt to the behavior of the less knowledgeable side, or (b) the knowledgeable side can push the other side to follow the knowledgeable side's behavior.
- If **both sides have basic knowledge of the other side's culture**, it is possible to approach each other in a coordinated way in which each side can adapt to the behavior of the other side to some extent.
- If **both sides are very familiar with each other's culture**, they can improvise. Depending on the situation, they can make the relationship work in the best possible way.

In any case, it is advisable to prepare well for negotiations with international partners. Familiarize yourself with their cultural background and study the negotiation customs of the countries involved. What are the specific circumstances of the negotiation? Who will take part? What is your relationship with the participants of the negotiation, both on a personal and professional level?

You should also be aware of your own behavior in negotiations (see the exercise below).

Appreciating your negotiating partners as human beings, searching for common ground, using active listening, clearing up misunderstandings, and being flexible are always helpful. Don't be upset when unexpected events occur, but use them as an opportunity to find new, creative solutions instead.

EXERCISE

YOUR OWN NEGOTIATION BEHAVIOR

- **Step 1:** Take a look at the possible characteristics of negotiation behavior according to Usunier again. Which behavioral tendencies can you identify in yourself?
- **Step 2:** How would you feel if you encountered different negotiation behaviors to the ones you are familiar and comfortable with? Is there development potential for you here in understanding and dealing with these other types of negotiation behavior? If this is the case, please make a note and add a corresponding activity to your personal development plan.
- **Step 3:** Discuss with your friends, colleagues, or fellow students how they behave in negotiations. You can also try to engage in a trial negotiation on any issue that is important to you. Then discuss how you felt about each other's negotiation behavior.

Conflicts in an intercultural environment

Life will always involve conflict, and life in an intercultural environment even more so. As people differ in their values and worldviews, conflicts over goals and relationships may occur more frequently and be more intense than in a non-intercultural environment.

Different cultures perceive conflict differently. While individualistic cultures tend to view conflict as a contest over ideas and goals, collectivist countries tend to view it as an absence of harmony.

When the parties involved are open with each other, and when they have an **independent sense of self** (that's the tendency to define yourself as separate from the social context), they might see conflict as an opportunity that produces creative solutions. Those who have an **interdependent sense of self** (that's the tendency to define yourself strongly through your association with a group) tend to shy away from conflict. For them, it is important that the parties involved in a conflict save face. We can find people with an independent or interdependent sense of self in all cultures. However, individualistic countries tend to have more people with an independent sense of self, and collectivist countries tend to have more people with an interdependent sense of self.[15]

People in a **low-context environment** tend to openly and explicitly address conflicts. They argue rationally and straightforwardly, and pursue open, direct strategies. In contrast, people in a **high-context environment** tend to address conflicts in a more implicit way. They argue intuitively and selectively, and pursue more ambiguous, indirect strategies.[16]

Kenneth W. Thomas investigated which **conflict resolution strategies** people usually follow and arranged them into two dimensions.[17] The first dimension is **assertiveness**, which can be defined as the extent to which the parties involved want to assert their own interests. The second dimension is **cooperativeness**, which is the extent to which the people involved are willing to include the other side in their deliberations.

Based on these two dimensions and building on Robert R. Blake and Jane S. Mouton's taxonomy of approaches to conflict management,[18] Thomas identified the following five **conflict resolution strategies**:[19]

- **Avoiding** (*low assertiveness* and *low willingness to cooperate*). The parties involved appear rather passive. They do not openly address the conflict, but instead suppress it, for example, by downplaying its importance. In this way, they do not really resolve the conflict.
- **Competing** (*high assertiveness* and *low willingness to cooperate*). The parties involved try to enforce their own position. They try to overcome resistance through arguments, threats, and underhanded tactics.
- **Compromising** (*medium assertiveness* and *medium willingness to cooperate*). The parties involved seek agreement. In doing so, they

partly give up their original positions and take the interests of the other party into account as far as possible.

- **Collaborating** (*high assertiveness* and *high willingness to cooperate*). The parties involved try to take each other's interests into account, but at the same time pursue their own interests as well. Respect and trust motivate their behavior. The parties involved exchange information and jointly seek solutions.
- **Accommodating** (*low assertiveness* and *high willingness to cooperate*). The parties involved put their own interests aside in favor of the other party and make concessions.

Even though you might find a general tendency toward a particular conflict resolution style in a culture, it does not mean that each individual will also use this style. Be prepared to encounter behavior that deviates from the rule. If you are aware of these basic conflict resolution strategies, however, and if you are able to recognize when someone is using a certain strategy, it will be easier for you to adapt your behavior to it.

EXERCISE

HOW DO YOU HANDLE CONFLICTS?

Try to find answers to the following questions:

- What does conflict mean to you? Is creating harmony or finding a creative solution more important to you?
- Which of Thomas's conflict resolution strategies suits you best? Are you able and willing to adopt other conflict resolution strategies too?
- Do you recognize which conflict resolution strategies other people follow?
- Can you deal with another strategy appropriately if it differs from your preferred one?

If you identify any development potential for yourself when answering these questions, include an appropriate action for further developing your conflict management skills in your personal development plan.

How to go on from here

Having taken a look at several additional aspects of intercultural sensitivity and competence, we will now come back to the idea of setting up a plan for taking your abilities to the next level. But let us first quickly talk about the baseline for all your actions in an intercultural environment: adopting an **intercultural mindset**.

Develop your intercultural mindset

Openness, curiosity, and **tolerance** are probably the most important traits for establishing a strong foundation for successful intercultural communication. In the course of this book, you have also become familiar with additional characteristics that together describe a general attitude that fosters effective intercultural communication.

Nowadays, we speak of a **mindset** to describe this general attitude.[20] Whenever you meet other people, try to remember to act according to an intercultural mindset. After each encounter, reflect on to what extent you have succeeded in maintaining this mindset.

The more often you consciously think about it, the faster this mindset will become familiar to you. Eventually, it will become second nature, and you will no longer have to think about it consciously. Other people will begin to sense your mindset, and may well tell you that you transmit openness and approachability.

What does openness, curiosity, and tolerance look like 'in practice'? How do you create this basis for effective communication with people from different cultural backgrounds?

Consider the following **tips for establishing your intercultural mindset**:

- **Treat all people as equals**, do not jump to conclusions about the motive behind an action and do not misinterpret their actions as being their personal characteristics.
- **Be tolerant and try to accept other opinions and ways of acting.** In every opinion, and in almost every action, there can be something positive. Try to find it! It is precisely from such a positive approach that very creative solutions can arise.

- **Be aware that the observations that you are making come from your perspective.** Other people may make very different observations from their own perspective, and that perspective can be just as 'correct' as yours. Try to see things from the perspective of other people, too. Why do they observe things differently to you? Why do they take a different position? Try to look at the world through their eyes. The more often and the more intensively you enter into interactions with people of different cultures, the easier it will become for you.
- **Don't let your internal 'classification machine' and stereotypes take over.** Recognize when they try to dominate you, think about them for a moment, consider why they are coming up at that particular moment, and then actively try to put them aside to have a free, unbiased view of your communication partner again.
- **Remember that all people enter communication situations with their own specific needs.** Try to recognize these needs and take them into account as much as possible.
- **Last but not least: don't give up.** If something hasn't worked out the way you wanted it to, think about what could be the underlying reasons. (We discussed a range of different reflection tools in Chapter 4—apply them, learn from the situation, and try to make it better next time.)

Taking the next steps

We have already discussed a few suggestions for developing your intercultural competencies in this book (for an overview in relation to culture shock, leadership, negotiations and conflicts, see the Table 1).

Aspect of cross-cultural competence	Culture shock	Leadership	Negotiations	Conflicts
Cognitive	Five-stages model	General characteristics of good leaders	Specifics of negotiations in your host country	Conflict resolution strategies
Behavioral	Strategies for dealing with these stages	Your own behavior as a leader	Your own negotiation behavior and the ability to switch between different negotiation styles	Your own conflict resolution style; adapting your own style to the current conflict situation
Affective	Be prepared for emotional reactions	Your emotional reactions to unfamiliar environments	How to handle uncertainty and other negotiation styles (especially those that are different from your own)	Your own emotions connected with conflicts; do not let them interfere with the conflict resolution process

Table 1 Overview of how key topics in this chapter are connected with intercultural competence

I am sure that you will already have many ideas about how you could further develop your intercultural sensitivity, but let me try to quickly summarize a few general strategies here.

Stay in other countries as often and as long as possible. I am not talking about tourist trips or vacations here. Try to live in other countries and, if possible, also study or work there. There are many opportunities to do this. Maybe you have already spent a year abroad as part of your school education. Some people spend a voluntary social gap year abroad. Programs like 'Global Work and Travel' allow you to experience another country from a completely new perspective, including both its work culture and its nature, history, and tourist hotspots. Maybe your university allows you to spend a semester abroad, or you could take on an overseas role in your company for a while? You might also want to organize a stay abroad on your own. (Many of my own students spend a semester abroad and then continue to experience the local work culture with an internship in that country.)

At your university or in your neighborhood, there will be **organizations that support foreign citizens** (e.g. for migrants, refugees, or guest students, to name just a few groups). You could offer help to these organizations, get socially involved, and gain intercultural experience at the same time. (Our university, for example, organizes a buddy program for students from other countries who spend their semesters abroad with us.)

Aim to **learn foreign languages**. On the one hand, language learning groups are very often culturally mixed. And on the other hand, languages transmit a lot of implicit knowledge about another culture. Besides that, you will usually also gain a lot of explicit information about the culture of the countries where the respective language is spoken.

Of course, formal **intercultural training** is another way of developing intercultural sensitivity. Maybe there are additional offerings at your university? Check the offers of the local language learning center. Sometimes, language courses implicitly include intercultural training, such as a course on negotiation techniques in English which is offered at our university.

Create your personal development plan

Now it's time to take one more step forward. In this section, I will invite you to create **your own personal plan for developing your level of intercultural sensitivity to a higher level**.

You will define your overall goal, think about the actions that can help you reach this goal, formulate them in a 'SMART' way, and then include them in a concrete action plan.

The template that you can find in Figure 14 (which you can also download from the companion website of this book at *www.econcise.com/ CulturalSensitivityTraining*) will guide you through this process.

Edwin A. Locke and Gary P. Latham argue that goals motivate us to accomplish things—but only if they are both challenging and achievable.[21] The goal should have a clear purpose and meaning for you: a 'why' that is guiding your actions.

Start with your own 'why' and think about what reaching the goal of developing your intercultural competence to a higher level would mean to you. Why do you want to achieve it?

Use the exercise below to set your goals and create a concrete action plan to achieve them.

CREATE YOUR PERSONAL DEVELOPMENT PLAN

Step 1: Your overall goal

Think about your overall goal—why would you like to develop your intercultural sensitivity? Do you want to prepare for a semester abroad or an expatriate assignment, or work in an intercultural team? Do you want to successfully complete your course at university? Or do you have other challenges in mind for which you need to develop intercultural sensitivity? If you are not clear about your personal goal yet, you might want to browse through this book again. In many places, you will find hints about the potential benefits of developing intercultural sensitivity. Discuss your thoughts with your friends, colleagues, or fellow students.

Write down your overall goal for developing your cross-cultural sensitivity in part 1 of the template in Figure 14.

Step 2: Compare your goal with your current situation

Now let's try to determine where you need to enhance your intercultural sensitivity to achieve your goal.

Take a sheet of paper and label the left third with "Where am I today?" and the right third with "Where do I want to go?" (See part 2 of the template in Figure 14.) Take a look at the first few exercises in this chapter again for inspiration for the "Where am I today?" column. Now think about where you would like to be in terms of your intercultural sensitivity by a certain point in time (e.g. the beginning of your semester abroad) and add this in the "Where do I want to go?" column.

Try to match the entries in the two columns now. Connect the points where you are already fulfilling or exceeding your expectations with a green line. Connect all other points that belong together with a red line. If on the right side there are some remaining points for which you do not find any entries on the left, then add a note about your current state to the left side. If your current state meets or exceeds your goal, use a green line to connect the state and the goal; otherwise use a red line.

Step 3: Derive actions

You will now probably have some red lines between the two columns. For each of these, think about actions you can take to get from your current state to your target state for that particular point. Write down all the actions you can and want to take to achieve your individual goals (see part 3 of the template in Figure 14).

Step 4: Formulate SMART goals

You have probably already heard that goals should be formulated in a SMART way.[22] Try to develop a SMART goal for each action that you have written down in the previous step.

As a reminder, here's how you can formulate goals in a SMART way:

- Be **specific**. What exactly do you want to achieve? (What is *not* part of your goal?)
- Set a **measurable** goal. This can be a bit difficult in the field of intercultural competencies. Research is still being conducted on the measurability of intercultural competencies, and there is no generally accepted measurement tool yet. However, you can consider how you can recognize if and how far your intercultural sensitivity has developed. Make a note about what you would consider to be your yardstick.
- Make sure that your goal is **achievable**, but don't make it too easy! Leave yourself a bit of a challenge, so that the goal will be motivating for you.
- Check if your goal is **relevant**. Ask yourself again why you want to achieve the goal (see step 1). Dig a bit deeper here: don't just say that you would like to "prepare for your semester abroad," but think about *why* you want to do that and why it is important for you.
- Finally, set yourself a **timeframe** by which you would like to have achieved your goal. Make sure that the deadline is achievable and realistic.

Step 5: Compiling the final plan

List all the SMART goals and actions in the order of their target date. Consider how long you will need to complete the individual actions. Add this information to the template (see parts 3 and 4 of the template in Figure 14). Will it be possible for you to complete all the actions by your planned target dates? Remember that you not only want to develop your intercultural sensitivity during this time, but will have other tasks to complete too. Make adjustments if necessary. You could, for example, postpone or cut lower priority tasks, or maybe include them within other, more encompassing tasks.

Step 6: Generating commitment for your plan

Stop! Before you let your plan disappear in a drawer or some folder on your computer, make sure that you will actually start working on it. Make it obligatory for yourself. What would such a commitment mean to you? Is it enough to tell your friends about it? Do you need a small ritual for it, e.g. toasting to the start of the plan with someone? Does it help if you are regularly reminded of your plan? You can reserve regular time slots in your calendar to work on your plan. You might also sign up right now for the language course that is part of your plan.

Think about how you can get feedback about your progress in implementing the plan. How will you measure success? How will you know whether you have achieved important milestones (see also step 3 above regarding making your goals measurable)? Both commitment and feedback are highly important for keeping you motivated so you will actually achieve your goals. Make a note about how you want to get feedback in part 5 of the template in Figure 14.

TEMPLATE FOR YOUR PERSONAL DEVELOPMENT PLAN

(1) Overall goal

_____

_____

(2)

Where am I today?   Where do I want to go?

_____   _____

_____   _____

_____   _____

_____   _____

(3) For all red lines

Where do I want to go (SMART)?	How do I want to get there?	Deadline

(4) Timeline

today   +1 week   +2 weeks   +3 weeks   +4 weeks   +5 weeks   +6 weeks
|————|————|————|————|————|————|———— ...

(5) How do I get feedback?

_____

_____

Figure 14 Template for creating your personal development plan

Congratulations! Through reading this book and completing the exercises in it you've already made great progress in developing your intercultural sensitivity. Now make a start on the plan you've just worked out and enjoy taking your intercultural sensitivity to the next level.

I wish you a lot of fun and success on your journey across the world, and above all I hope you have enriching and rewarding intercultural encounters!

KEY TAKEAWAYS FROM CHAPTER 5

1. Developing cultural and intercultural sensitivity is an **ongoing process**.

2. It may be necessary to **improve additional aspects of your own cultural sensitivity** in order to have positive encounters with an unfamiliar culture.

3. Being in contact with a **diverse network of people** provides you with constant training opportunities for developing your cultural sensitivity.

4. **Travel, travel, travel**—preferably with intensive direct contact with local people.

5. Languages implicitly carry cultural interpretations and values. **Learning languages** enhances your sense of cultural diversity and will help you come into more direct contact with local people.

6. A sound **development plan** will help you to further follow your path toward interesting and enriching intercultural encounters.

Notes for Chapter 5

1   Bennett (1986; 1993).
2   The following section is inspired by ideas in Bennett (1986; 1993).
3   Salovey and Mayer (1990).
4   Bolten (2012).
5   Ibarra (2015).
6   Oberg (1960).
7   Ibid.
8   Dekker (2016).
9   Ferraro (2010).
10 House et al. (2004).
11 Ibid.
11 Deresky (2016).
12 Usunier (2003).
13 Weiss (1994).
14 Ibid.
15 Ting-Tommey (1999).
16 Gudykunst et al. (1985).
17 Thomas (1990).
18 Blake and Mouton (1994).
19 Thomas (1990).
20 Dekker (2016).
21 Locke and Latham (2002).
22 Drucker (1977).

A concluding note

Before you continue your intercultural journey, let's take a quick look back at what tools and knowledge you now have to help you on your way:

- You are now aware of the **automatic reactions** that nature has given us, what they sometimes tempt us to do, and how you can actively deal with them.
- You know different **cultural systems**, which will help you to make a first general assessment of people from other cultures. You have already tried this out by taking a closer look at your own cultural background.
- You also understand the role of **personal characteristics, motivation, and discussion styles** in intercultural encounters. In this context, you have got to know your 'inner team,' which you carry with you wherever you go.
- Other tools will help you **prepare for critical intercultural situations**, or reflect in retrospect on what went wrong and what you would like to do differently in such situations in the future.
- Last but not least, you have outlined the next steps of your journey by **planning how to reach the next level of your intercultural competence**.

If you feel this book has helped you to better understand your own cultural background as well as how to survive and thrive in intercultural situations, I would really be happy if you could write a short, honest online review about the book. This will help other people to find it, and the more people develop their intercultural sensitivity, the more pleasant, enriching, and rewarding intercultural encounters we will have in our world.

Thank you for embarking on this adventure toward greater intercultural sensitivity; it was a pleasure for me to accompany you on this journey.

List of references

Allport, G. W., & Odbert, H. S. (1936). Trait-names: A psycho-lexical study. *Psychological Monographs, 47*(1), i-171.

Baumeister, R. F., & Leary, M. R. (1995). The need to belong: Desire for interpersonal attachments as a fundamental human motivation. *Psychological Bulletin, 117*(3), 497–529.

Bennett, M. J. (1986). A developmental approach to training for intercultural sensitivity. *International Journal of Intercultural Relations, 10*(2), 179–196.

Bennett, M. J. (1993). Towards ethnorelativism: A developmental model of intercultural sensitivity (revised). In Paige, R. M. (ed.), *Education for the Intercultural Experience* (pp. 21–72). Boston, MA: Intercultural Press Inc.

Blake, R. R., & Mouton, J. S. (1994). *The Managerial Grid* (Paperback rerelease of 1964 ed.). Houston, TX: Gulf Publishing.

Bolten, J. (2012). *Interkulturelle Kompetenz* (Neuaufl.). Erfurt: Landeszentrale für Politische Bildung Thüringen.

De Bono, E. (1992). *Six Thinking Hats*, revised and updated edition. London: Penguin Life.

Browaeys, M.-J., & Price, R. (2019). *Understanding Cross-Cultural Management*, 4th ed. Harlow: Pearson Education Limited.

Chhokar, J. S., Brodbeck, F. C., & House, R. J. (eds) (2019). *Culture and Leadership Across the World: The GLOBE Book of In-Depth Studies of 25 Societies*. Hove: Psychology Press.

Clear, J. (2018). *Atomic Habits: Tiny Changes, Remarkable Results; an Easy & Proven Way to Build Good Habits & Break Bad Ones*. New York, NY: Avery.

Daft, R. L., & Lengel, R. H. (1983). Information richness: A new approach to managerial behavior and organizational design. *Research in Organizational Behavior, 6*, 191–233.

Davidov, E. (2008). A cross-country and cross-time comparison of the human values measurements with the second round of the European Social Survey. *Survey Research Methods, 2* (1), 33-46.

Dekker, W. den. (2016). *Global Mindset and Cross-Cultural Behavior: Improving Leadership Effectiveness*. London: Palgrave Macmillan.

Dennis, A. R., & Valacich, J. S. (1999). Rethinking media richness: Towards a theory of media synchronicity. *Proceedings of the 32nd Annual Hawaii International Conference on Systems Sciences. 1999. HICSS-32. Abstracts and CD-ROM of Full Papers* (p. 10). IEEE Comput. Soc. https://doi.org/10.1109/HICSS.1999.772701

Deresky, H. (2016). *International Management*, 9th ed. Harlow: Pearson Education Limited.

Devine, P. G. (1989). Stereotypes and prejudice: Their automatic and controlled components. *Journal of Personality and Social Psychology, 56*(1), 5–18.

Drucker, P. F. (1977). *People and Performance: The Best of Peter Drucker on Management*. London: Heinemann.

Felmingham, K., Kemp, A., Williams, L., Das, P., Hughes, G., Peduto, A., & Bryant, R. (2007). Changes in anterior cingulate and amygdala after cognitive behavior therapy of posttraumatic stress disorder. *Psychological Science, 18*(2), 127–129.

Ferraro, G. P. (2010). *The Cultural Dimension of International Business,* 6th international ed. Harlow: Prentice Hall.

Festinger, L. (1962). Cognitive dissonance. *Scientific American, 207*(4), 93–102.

Fiske, S. T. (2018). Stereotype content: Warmth and competence endure. *Current Directions in Psychological Science, 27*(2), 67–73.

Fiske, S. T., Cuddy, A. J. C., Glick, P., & Xu, J. (2002). A model of (often mixed) stereotype content: Competence and warmth respectively follow from perceived status and competition. *Journal of Personality and Social Psychology, 82*(6), 878–902.

Fiske, S. T., & Neuberg, S. L. (1990). A continuum model of impression formation from category-based to individuating processing: Influences of information and motivation on attention and interpretation. In Zanna, M. P. (ed.), *Advances in Experimental and Social Psychology* (pp. 1-108). London: Academic Press.

Frankl, V. E., & Weigel, H. (2017). *… trotzdem Ja zum Leben sagen: Ein Psychologe erlebt das Konzentrationslager.* Munich: Penguin Verlag.

Gertsen, M. C. (1990). Intercultural competence and expatriates. *The International Journal of Human Resource Management, 1*(3), 341–362.

Goldberg, L. R. (1990). An alternative "description of personality": The big-five factor structure. *Journal of Personality and Social Psychology, 59*(6), 1216–1229.

Gruber, M. (2011). *Kritische Auseinandersetzung mit Hofstedes Konzept der Kulturstandards bzw. Kulturdimensionen.* Munich: GRIN Verlag GmbH.

Gudykunst, W. B., Stewart, L. P., & Ting-Toomey, S. (Eds.). (1985). *International and Intercultural Communication Annual: Vol. 9. Communication, Culture, and Organizational Processes.* Thousand Oaks, CA: SAGE Publications.

Hall, E. T. (1973). *The Silent Language: An Anthropologist Reveals How We Communicate by Our Manners and Behavior.* New York, NY: Anchor Press/Doubleday.

Hall, E. T. (1977). *Beyond Culture.* New York, NY: Anchor Press

Hall, E. T. (1982). *The Hidden Dimension.* New York, NY: Doubleday.

Hall, E. T., & Hall, M. R. (1990). *Understanding Cultural Differences.* Boston, MA: Intercultural Press.

Hofstede, G. (2001). *Culture's Consequences: Comparing Values, Behaviors, Institutions, and Organizations across Nations,* 2nd ed. Thousand Oaks, CA: SAGE Publications.

Hofstede, G., & Hofstede, G. J. (2006). *Lokales Denken, globales Handeln: Interkulturelle Zusammenarbeit und globales Management,* 3rd ed. Munich: DTV/ Beck.

Hofstede, G., Hofstede, G. J., & Minkov, M. (2010). *Cultures and Organizations: Software of the Mind; Intercultural Cooperation and its Importance for Survival,* 3rd ed. New York, NY: McGraw-Hill.

House, R. J. (ed.). (2004). *Culture, Leadership, and Organizations: The GLOBE study of 62 Societies.* Thousand Oaks, CA: SAGE Publications.

House, R. J., Dorfman, P. W., Javidan, M., Hanges, P. J., & Sully De Luque, Mary F. (2013). *Strategic Leadership Across Cultures: The GLOBE Study of CEO Leadership Behavior and Effectiveness in 24 Countries.* Thousand Oaks, CA: SAGE Publications.

Hucke, V. (2019). *Fair führen*. Frankfurt/Main: Campus Verlag.

Ibarra, H. (2015). *Act like a Leader, Think like a Leader*. Boston, MA: Harvard Business Review Press.

Inglehart, R. (2018). *Cultural Evolution: People's Motivations are Changing, and Reshaping the World*. Cambridge: Cambridge University Press.

Kahneman, D. (2012). *Thinking, Fast and Slow*. New York, NY: Penguin Books.

Kluckhohn, F. R., & Strodtbeck, F. L. (1961). *Variations in Value Orientations*. Evanston, IL: Row, Peterson.

Kumbier, D. (Ed.). (2006). *Interkulturelle Kommunikation: Methoden, Modelle, Beispiele*. Hamburg: Rowohlt-Taschenbuch-Verlag.

Lewis, R. D. (2018). *When Cultures Collide: Leading across Cultures*, 4th ed. Boston, MA: Nicholas Brealey Publishing.

Lipmann, W. (2018). *Public Opinion: How People Decide; The Role of News, Propaganda and Manufactured Consent in Modern Democracy and Political Elections*. Paris: Adansonia Publishing.

Locke, E. A., & Latham, G. P. (2002). Building a practically useful theory of goal setting and task motivation. A 35-year odyssey. *The American Psychologist, 57*(9), 705–717.

Martin, R. A. (2006). *The Psychology of Humor: An Integrative Approach*. Burlington, MA: Elsevier Academic Press.

Maslow, A. H. (1943). A theory of human motivation. *Psychological Review, 50*(4), 370–396.

McClelland, D. C. (1961). *The Achieving Society*. New York, NY: The Free Press.

Morgan, A. (2022). *Coaching International Teams*. Moosburg: econcise.

Nerdinger, F. W. (2012). *Grundlagen des Verhaltens in Organisationen*. Stuttgart: Verlag W. Kohlhammer.

Nevis, E. C. (1983). Using an American perspective in understanding another culture: Toward a hierarchy of needs for the People's Republic of China. *The Journal of Applied Behavioral Science, 19*(3), 249–264.

Neyer, F. J., & Asendorpf, J. B. (2018). *Psychologie der Persönlichkeit*, 6th ed. Berlin/Heidelberg: Springer

Oberg, K. (1960). Cultural shock: Adjustment to new cultural environments. *Practical Anthropology, 7*(4), 177–182.

Riemann, F. (2013). *Grundformen der Angst*, 41st ed. Munich: Ernst Reinhardt Verlag.

Ryan, R. M., & Deci, E. L. (2017). *Self-Determination Theory: Basic Psychological Needs in Motivation, Development, and Wellness*. New York, NY: The Guilford Press.

Salovey, P., & Mayer, J. D. (1990). Emotional intelligence. *Imagination, Cognition and Personality, 9*(3), 185–211.

Schneider, S. C., & Barsoux, J.-L. (2003). *Managing Across Cultures*, 2nd ed. Harlow: Pearson Education.

Schulz von Thun, F. (1981). *Störungen und Klärungen: Psychologie der zwischenmenschlichen Kommunikation*. Hamburg: Rowohlt-Taschenbuch-Verlag.

Schulz von Thun, F. (2013). *Das "Innere Team" und situationsgerechte Kommunikation: Kommunikation, Person, Situation*, 26th ed. Hamburg: Rowohlt Taschenbuch.

Schwartz, S. H. (2012). An overview of the Schwartz theory of basic values. *Online Readings in Psychology and Culture, 2*(1). https://doi.org/10.9707/2307-0919.1116

Thomann, C., & Schulz von Thun, F. (2003). *Handbuch für Therapeuten, Gesprächshelfer und Moderatoren in schwierigen Gesprächen*. Hamburg: Rowohlt-Taschenbuch-Verlag.

Thomas, A. (2003). Interkulturelle Kompetenz—Grundlagen, Probleme und Konzepte. *Erwägen, Wissen, Ethik, 14*(1), 37–228.

Thomas, K. W. (1990). Conflict and negotiation processes in organizations. In Dunnette, M. D., Hough, L. M., & Triandis, H. C. (eds), *Handbook of Industrial and Organizational Psychology*, 2nd ed. (pp. 651–717). Palo Alto, CA: Consulting Psychologists Press.

Ting-Toomey, S. (1999). *Communicating Across Cultures*. New York, NY: Guilford Press.

Trompenaars, F., & Hampden-Turner, C. (1998). *Riding the Waves of Culture: Understanding Cultural Diversity in Global Business*, 2nd ed. New York, NY: McGraw Hill.

Turner, J. C. (1987). *Rediscovering the Social Group: A Self-Categorization Theory*. Oxford: Basil Blackwell.

Usunier, J.-C. (2003). Cultural aspects of international business negotiations. In Ghauri, P. N. & Usunier. J.-C. (eds), *International Business Negotiations*, 2nd ed. (pp. 91–118). Boston, MA: Pergamon.

Wegener, D. T., & Petty, R. E. (1997). The flexible correction model: The role of naive theories of bias in bias correction. In Zann, M. P. (ed.), *Advances in Experimental Social Psychology, Vol. 29* (pp. 141–208). Amsterdam: Elsevier.

Weiss, S. E. (1994). Negotiating with "Romans"—Part 1. *Sloan Management Review, 35*(2), 51–61.

Yoshino, K., & Smith, C. (2013). *Uncovering Talent: A New Model of Inclusion*. Deloitte LLP/ Deloitte University.

Index

Locke, Edwin A. 165
long-term orientation 37-8
love needs 75
low-context cultures 115, 160

M

Martin, Rod 132
masculinity 35-6, 80
Maslow, Abraham H. 74
McClelland, David C. 72, 74
meaning 77
    of work 78
media richness theory 125
media synchronicity theory 125
medium of communication 124-5
meta-communication 136
monochronic societies 53, 111
Morgan, Alexandra 128
motivation 68-9, 173
    in the workplace 77
motives 69, 71
multi-active societies 55
multiculturalism 14, 15

N

national culture 14
need
    for achievement 72-3
    for affiliation 72-3
    for power 72
    for self-actualization 75
needs 72-74
    according to Maslow 74
    according to McClelland 72
negotiation 156-9
network of contacts 150
Neuberg, Steven 9, 10, 21
neuroticism (personality trait) 83
Nevis, Edward 75
norms 16

O

OCEAN model 82
openness (personality trait) 82
organizational culture 13

P

paternalistic stereotypes 17
performance orientation (cultural
    dimension) 45
personal characteristics *see personality
    traits*
personal development plan 165
    exercise 166
    template 169
personality 81
    model ('Big Five') 82
    traits 81-4, 95
personal space 122-4
physical touch 123
physiological needs 75
polychronic societies 53, 111
Portrait Values Questionnaire 44
power (cultural dimension) 42
power distance 32-3, 46, 79
power relations 5
professional culture 13
proximity orientation 86
pyramid of needs 74-6

R

racism 5, 11, 16
reactive societies 55
reflection 25-6, 148
regulation 69, 70
relationship to the environment 51
resolving critical situations *see resol-
    ving difficult situations*
resolving difficult interactions *see
    resolving difficult situations*

Dr. Susann Kowalski is a professor at TH Köln University of Applied Sciences and has been teaching courses in intercultural competencies and management, as well as personal development, at both undergraduate and graduate levels for over 20 years. She has years of experience teaching interculturally mixed groups of students in Germany as well as in countries as diverse as India, Russia, China, and the USA.

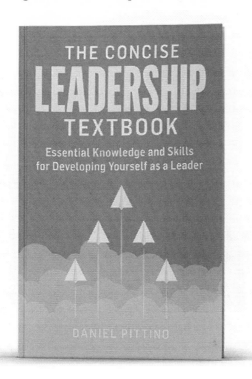

Made in United States
Troutdale, OR
07/21/2023

11455031R10118